Academic Interactions:
Communicating on Campus

Christine B. Feak, Susan M. Reinhart, & Theresa N. Rohlck
University of Michigan

Michigan Series in English for
Academic & Professional Purposes
Series Editors: John M. Swales & Christine B. Feak

Ann Arbor
The University of Michigan Press

Copyright © by the University of Michigan 2009
All rights reserved
Published in the United States of America
The University of Michigan Press
Manufactured in the United States of America

♾ Printed on acid-free paper

ISBN-13: 978-0-472-03332-4

2012   2011   2010   2009   4   3   2   1

Acknowledgments

Thanks to Others

No book can be created without the support and input from many others. We would like to take this opportunity to acknowledge all who have contributed to our effort.

First of all, we would like to express our thanks to the three anonymous reviewers who gave us insightful feedback and suggestions that have helped shape the final version of this book. In addition to the reviewers, we'd like to acknowledge the efforts of those who read and in some cases trialed early versions of the material: Margo Czinski, Sonya Choi, and Tanya Sydorenko.

Closer to home we need to recognize the support of the English Language Institute and our many colleagues there. In particular, ELI Director Steven Dworkin who provided some financial resources for the production of the DVD; Sheryl Leicher for her early MICASE materials development that helped point us in the right direction; our librarian Benedette Palazzola and library assistant Kimberly Hoff; Diane Larsen-Freeman, who gave us advice on grammar; Brenda Imber and Pamela Bogart, who graciously gave of their time and pronunciation expertise when we were struggling with that part of the book; Rachel Wilson, for her work on the transcripts of the DVD scenes; Lisa Russ for all the moral support along the way; Barb Dobson for her input on transcript use and her sympathetic ear (as a seasoned author herself); and finally, we owe a debt of gratitude to John Swales, who has for many years supported our textbook writing endeavors and whose input on this project has been invaluable.

Over the years our students have been major contributors: they told us what worked, what didn't work, what was interesting, what was boring, and what made no sense whatsoever. We appreciate their willingness to try out new materials and give us their feedback.

For the filming and production of the DVD, a huge thank you goes to Elie Mosseri of Mosseri Enterprises, and his crew, Ruben Rodriguez (video) and Doug Trevethan (audio). Their positive attitude, enthusiasm, patience, and attention to detail went beyond our expectations. And above all, we really appreciate the fact that they did everything with a great sense of humor.

Of course, without actors, there would be no DVD. Our heartfelt thanks and appreciation to our family members, former students, and friends, who (with extraordinary good humor and patience) contributed their time and talent to this project.

Jean Campbell	Vera Irwin
Jake Christensen	Sun Hyun Park
Angie Feak	Morgan Peterson
Karl Feak	Robin Reinhart
Darnell Forte	Lb Rohlck
Chuang Chung Hu	

Finally, we are indebted to Kelly Sippell, our editor, who encouraged us to write the text and wholly supported the project from its initial stages to its completion, including the addition of a DVD to supplement the text. Her patience in what became a quite lengthy process is also very much appreciated.

On a more personal note, Chris would like to thank Glen, Karl, and Angie who, once again, endured the uncertainty of her schedule and endless "spaghetti dinners" so that this book could come to fruition. Theresa would like to thank Carolyn Madden for her continued support and past collaboration that has informed parts of this project; and Mario and Ayi, for having to watch countless Tigers and Wings games without her, but always letting her know the scores while she was still at the office working. Sue dedicates this book to her brother Charles for his support over the years.

Grateful acknowledgment is made to the following authors, publishers, and individuals for permission to use their materials.

Pamela Bogart for the use of her PowerPoint slides.

Bei Huang for use of her ELI 334: Academic Speaking class presentation Q&A.

Prospective Students Advisory Committee, Office of College Admissions, University of Chicago, for permission to use a condensed version of Apratim Sahay's student profile found on the Prospective Students Advisory Committee website.

The University of Michigan, English Language Institute, for permission to use MICASE transcript excerpts.

The University of Michigan ELI 530: Academic Speaking and Writing for Architecture Students class, Fall 2007, for class discussion (Chuang-Chung, Yongha, Kwangseok, Jaehyung, YS, Richard, and guests).

Contents

Introduction

This speaking book is aimed at high-intermediate to advanced students who are either in an intensive academic English program or have newly begun their academic careers at a U.S. community college, college, or university at either the undergraduate or graduate level.

The material in this book is the result of a materials development project (of nearly ten years) based on our experiences teaching academic speaking courses in both the regular academic year and the pre-sessional summer programs at the English Language Institute. The goal of these courses—as well as the materials that have emerged from them—is to help students whose first language is not English acquire some of the basic communication skills they need to be successful in a college or university setting. These skills include giving directions, writing effective email messages, participating in class discussions and office hours as well as giving a group presentation, to name a few.

We have taken what we consider to be the best of our material and created six units. Each of the units, except for Unit 3 on email, which, of course, is not considered a spoken genre, relies heavily on transcripts of actual academic speaking events, particularly classroom interactions and office hours. These transcripts are part of the Michigan Corpus of Academic Spoken English (MICASE, pronounced as my-case), an invaluable resource that contains transcripts and recordings of 200 hours (approximately 1.8 million words) of academic speech from across the University of Michigan campus. Each unit has at least one focus on language use, ranging from ellipsis to the language of apologies to hedging. The language focus topics were chosen based on our analyses of the MICASE transcripts as well as our own small corpus of email messages. In addition to the consistent use of MICASE, we have attempted to use published research as much as possible to inform our materials development. In doing so, we hope that we have provided more accurate explanations of how language is actually used and what the expectations of the academic community are, rather than basing our discussion on guesswork and intuition. Other features to be found in each of the units are outlines of learning goals at the beginning, text analysis, and a major speaking activity or, as in the case of the email unit, email writing activities.

A DVD accompanies this text; the DVD is not sold separately. It includes scenes of academic interactions relevant to each unit, such as giving or asking for directions for Unit 1 and for Unit 4 office hour interactions. The DVD also contains other supplementary material such as examples of gestures and body language, which are important for effective communication. In addition to DVD scenes, each unit includes a brief pronunciation focus section. To supplement each unit, a short reading topically related to each unit can be found in the Instructor's Notes, available on the Internet.

Organization

Unit 1 focuses on names and places. This unit offers students opportunities to learn about proper names in the United States, to practice giving directions, and to prepare an informal group presentation.

Unit 2 gives students a chance to understand who their college professors are and what their expectations of students may be.

Unlike the other units that focus on speaking, Unit 3 deals with the challenges of email, including subject headings, greetings, and politeness, among other important aspects of electronic communication.

The emphasis in Unit 4 is office hours. The unit begins by discussing the reasons students go to office hours and then takes a close look at what goes on in office hour interactions by looking at several transcripts of typical student-instructor interactions.

In Unit 5, students learn about class participation. This unit delves into why and how students do or do not participate in class along with what instructors do to encourage participation. The unit closes with a look at the role of personal narratives in the classroom.

The final unit centers on seminar style discussion and a more formal panel presentation. Key aspects of this unit include the language of opinions and interruptions, paraphrasing and summary, and discourse strategies that contribute to a successful panel presentation (e.g., overviews and transitions between speakers). Although there are many other topics we could have chosen, we selected these because our students report having significant difficulty with them. Instructor's Notes are available on the University of Michigan Press website.

Working with Transcripts and MICASE

One of the central features of this textbook is the emphasis on authentic language used in an academic setting rather than fabricated examples of language use in a particular context. We are able to provide examples of authentic use thanks to the availability of MICASE. MICASE is publicly available at http://quod.lib.umich.edu/m/micase/. In some cases, sound files are also available for the recorded speech events. To a lesser degree we have also incorporated examples of authentic language from recordings of our own classes.

The use of authentic language examples is not without its drawbacks, however. Problems can arise because everyday spoken language does not necessarily consist of complete, well-formed sentences; nor does it necessarily flow smoothly. To address these issues, the transcripts of the excerpts we have chosen for the text have, for the most part, been edited or slightly revised from the MICASE version, usually in order to increase readability and clarity. In doing so, we have made every effort to remain true to the spirit of the transcripts while editing the language and adapting content to make them more accessible. By focusing on whether the transcript could be understood as opposed to being grammatically correct, we hope that students will gain confidence in their speaking by realizing that in many speaking contexts there is a high tolerance for false starts, incomplete utterances, grammar errors, and unusual word choices. Another bit of editing we have done on the original transcripts has to do with punctuation. Transcription conventions for MICASE include the use of familiar punctuation marks in unfamiliar ways; thus, one way we have edited the transcripts is to make the punctuation more consistent with standard use (commas for pauses, periods for ends of thought groups). We have also tried to keep to a more standard use of capitalization. In addition, we have added (fictional) names for speakers when it seemed helpful to understanding the interactions. We used the MICASE convention of identifying speakers by number (S1, S2, S3) in some transcripts. Embedded or overlapping speech is indicated within brackets and occurs within the main speaker's words. For example, **Ann:** I'll install the new software if you want me to [**Nadeen:** Really?] but I can't do it until tomorrow.

MICASE is also important to this text because our choices of what to teach and discussions of how language is used are informed and supported by research, and not solely based on our own intuitions. In doing research on the database, we have found that our intuitions of language use (and those represented in many other speaking books) are often incorrect. For instance, our intuition may tell us that in order to make a suggestion, the verb *suggest* is rather important. However, a look at MICASE reveals something very different. More useful than *suggest* is the expression *you might wanna*.

References to the MICASE transcripts on which our excerpts are based are given after each transcript. Instructors and students can and should access the MICASE to further investigate academic spoken language or to look at the complete speech event. By searching MICASE, students can zero in on field- or discipline-specific speech events that may be of interest to them. Students may also want to record and transcribe some of their own speech; this can be accomplished by going to the MICASE website and clicking the link to a free software program called "Soundscriber," which has features that make transcribing recorded speech quite manageable. We also suggest that instructors visit MICASE to create additional tasks for their students. To facilitate this process, suggestions for browsing and searching are available on the MICASE website. More in-depth discussion of how to use MICASE can also be found in *The MICASE Handbook: A Resource for Users of the Michigan Corpus for Academic Spoken English* (Simpson-Vlach and Leicher 2006) published by the University of Michigan Press.

In our own classes at the University of Michigan's English Language Institute, we frequently incorporate MICASE. We have found that it does in fact take some effort to become comfortable working with transcripts, for both instructors and students. However, after the initial time spent becoming accustomed to reading and analyzing transcripts, the results are highly rewarding.

We have tried to carefully choose the transcripts so that the content does not "get in the way" or cause students to lose focus of the language or important aspects of the speech event illustrated by the transcript. However, spending a few moments before working with a transcript to clarify any unusual vocabulary or content will be time well spent. And it is our hope that student questions about the transcripts, content, or context will provide starting points for valuable discussion and speaking practice. This can be a blessing and a curse—any one transcript could potentially provide hours of classroom material, depending on the focus (vocabulary, speaker roles/status, idiomatic expressions, politeness, pronunciation, word stress and pausing, turn taking, cultural differences, and so on).

We are frequently asked how we present the dialogues and interactions in the transcripts in class without an audio file of the transcript. What we do depends on a number of factors, and there is no single approach that will work well for every transcript. When planning to use a transcript, you need to consider the topic, the length, the number of speakers, the number of turns, and other characteristics of the speaking event.

We have done all of the following approaches in our teaching.

- Students role-play the interaction.
- The instructor reads the parts out loud.
- The instructor and student(s) read the parts out loud.
- Partners or small groups read through/role-play in their own groups.
- Students read through a transcript before class so that class time can focus on the questions and discussion.
- Students read or role-play with a native speaker of English outside of class.
- The instructor prepares an in-house recording for use in class.

Because working through transcripts can take time, some other strategies we use include breaking longer transcripts into chunks and working through relevant questions, such as Lines 1 to 10 and Questions 1 to 3 and dividing questions among smaller groups or pairs of students so each group has one question to prepare and then makes a report to the class.

We have found that it is hard to get back into a transcript activity that was left unfinished at the end of one class. Because momentum is hard to regain, we plan strategic stopping points in the units rather than find ourselves with a lengthy transcript only "half-done."

This volume is the first academic speaking book in which transcripts of authentic spoken English are central. We hope that we have made good transcript and other content choices. We would be most interested in learning the ways in which you use the transcripts as well, and would welcome an email message from you describing what you have done; email us at esladmin@umich.edu.

The DVD

During the planning of this book, we decided that students could gain a better understanding of the language used in academic settings if, in addition to the transcripts in the texts, we provided some video and/or audio examples of key academic interactions, such as office hours and group meetings. In order to demonstrate how different kinds of interaction unfold and to enhance the learning experience of students, we decided to produce a DVD to complement the material in the book. We had initially thought that we would semi-script the DVD scenes in order to have some control over the content and language. This, however, proved to be difficult because it would have required the creation of scripts, multiple rehearsals for our volunteer actors, and memorization of scripts. We abandoned this plan in part because of scheduling constraints but mainly because we found that many of our scene topics were relatively easy to role-play as long as the actors had experience with the kinds of situations that we wanted to capture on the DVD. In the end, we decided to bring in the camera crew, assign our actors to specific scenes (taking into consideration their individual backgrounds and strengths), and then let the actors play out the designated scenes as they wanted. In other words, the scenes are improvised, based on some limited guidance from us, such as asking an actor to try using *you might wanna* when giving advice or asking the actor to be inconsiderate during the office hour scene. As a result of this process, the language of the DVD is unscripted and contains all of the usual characteristics of spoken language: false starts, hesitations, repetitions, "errors," and so on. As a result, we are confident that the material on the DVD mirrors actual language in typical academic interactions and provides students with relevant examples of common situations that students are likely to encounter.

We have used the DVD in a number of ways beyond reinforcing the material in the book. The various scenes can be used—with or without the transcripts—to:

- practice pronunciation (see more specific suggestions in the Pronunciation Focus section on p. xiv)
- work on listening comprehension
- illustrate grammar
- work on vocabulary building
- discuss slang and idiomatic expressions
- provide a springboard for discussion
- illustrate aspects of U.S. culture
- highlight examples of nonverbal communication (gestures and body language)
- focus on active listening strategies
- compare and contrast different versions of similar academic interactions (for instance, office hours).

Additional suggestions for using the DVD as well as the transcripts for each of the scenes can be found on the University of Michigan Press website (www.press.umich.edu/esl).

Pronunciation Focus Sections

Each unit contains a Pronunciation Focus designed to help students discover some guidelines for English pronunciation. Additional Pronunciation Focus sections can be found in the Instructor's Notes. In other books, typical pronunciation work begins with a rule and then gives students words or sentences to pronounce. In preparing pronunciation materials for our students, we found this approach to be problematic, especially because there is a fair amount of native speaker variation and because no single rule seems to work for all situations. So, rather than tell students what the "rules" for pronunciation are, we have set out tasks in which students transcribe short segments from DVD scenes and then write their observations based on what they hear. We think that having students note for themselves what is going on will be more interesting for them and give them a better sense of authentic American English pronunciation. If you want more pronunciation practice for your students, any of the transcripts in the text or Instructor's Notes can also provide a starting point. Some other Pronunciation Focus ideas you may wish to explore include asking students

- to mark the transcript for intonation
- to mark the transcript for chunks or thought groups and figure out where appropriate pauses occur.

You can also create pronunciation exercises by asking students to use transcripts

- to record themselves and compare to a recording of the same text by a native speaker
- to find instances of fast speech
- to identify chunks of language where words are likely blended together (e.g., *some money*).

UNIT

Names, Places, and Directions

In this first unit we'll begin by looking at names and places that may be important when interacting in the academic community. We'll also focus on giving and getting directions. By the end of the unit, you should be able to:

- describe how you got your name
- clearly pronounce the names of key places and people in your academic community
- understand and use common prepositions in giving and getting directions
- give directions to a particular location using landmarks as your guide
- recognize ellipsis in speaking
- describe the location and history of an important building in your community
- describe places or businesses in your community.

Let's begin by looking at people's names in the United States.

The Most Common Names in the United States

Naming practices are always changing. Many names that were popular 40 to 50 years ago are no longer fashionable, but some have maintained their popularity.

TABLE 1. Top 10 Names in the United States, 1950 and 2007

Rank	Male Name 1950	Male Name 2007	Female Name 1950	Female Name 2007
1	James	Jacob	Linda	Emily
2	Robert	Michael	Mary	Isabella
3	John	Ethan	Patricia	Emma
4	Michael	Joshua	Barbara	Ava
5	David	Daniel	Susan	Madison
6	William	Christopher	Nancy	Sophia
7	Richard	Anthony	Deborah	Olivia
8	Thomas	William	Sandra	Abigail
9	Charles	Matthew	Carol	Hannah
10	Gary	Andrew	Kathleen	Elizabeth

Popular Baby Names, *www.ssa.gov/OACT/babynames*. Accessed Feb. 1, 2008.

Task 1

Look at Table 1, and discuss the changes you notice in the ten most popular names given to boys and girls. Are you aware of any changes in popular names of different generations in other cultures or countries?

Task 2

Many people have stories to tell about how they were named. Some children are named after a relative, a close friend, or a famous person. In some cases, a given name might have simply been made up. In other cases, the name carries a particular meaning. Discuss with a partner or partners how your name was chosen and whether it has a particular meaning.

Did you choose a name that you use in your English language classes? If so, how did you choose it? Was it given by a teacher?

Here are some expressions that you might find useful in completing the task.

I was named after my (grandfather, grandmother, uncle, aunt).

My (grandfather, grandmother, uncle, aunt) named me/chose my name because . . . .

My name means . . . .

When parents choose names in my culture they . . .

Why Do Some People in the United States Have Three Names?

Many Americans have three names: a given name (first name), a middle name, and a sur-name (family name). While the tradition of having a first and last name may not need explaining, the purpose of a middle name may be less clear. Research shows that middle names were not commonly given until the 1800s, when German immigrants introduced the tradition to the United States. The use of the second given name was considered to be a sta-tus symbol. Although in the United States middle names were initially religious in nature, by the 1900s middle names were not connected to religion but often consisted of the mother's maiden name (Tracy 2007).

Do you have a middle name? If so, how was it chosen?

Nicknames

It is fairly common for people to be called by a nickname or short form of their given name. In the United States, for example, some people may be called by a shortened version of their name, often based on the first syllable but sometimes the second. Someone by the name of *Andrew* may go by *Andy* or *Drew*. *Andrea* can become *Andi* (or *Andy),* and *Nicholas* can become *Nick*. Other shortened versions are a result of a more dramatic change. For instance, someone with the given name *William* might be called *Bill*. A person with the given name *Kathleen* may be called *Kate, Katie,* or *Kathy*. Often you can use a person's nickname, provided that you notice that others refer to that person by that name or the person indicates that you should use the nickname. If, however, a person has a nickname that derives from personal characteristics or interests, you need to be more careful. A person with red hair may have the nickname *Red*, but most likely only those close to the person will use it.

Gender-Neutral First Names

Sometimes it is not clear whether a given name is male or female, which can cause confu-sion. According to a recent United States census, the given name *Chris* was statistically the most likely to be used for either males or females. Other names in the gender-neutral cate-gory include: *Taylor, Terry, Pat, Jesse,* and *Jamie*. Do you know of any others? How would you address someone whom you do not know with a gender-neutral name in a letter or email message?

DVD Task

Unit 1: Names

Scenes 1–3

In these scenes, three students are sharing stories about their own names—how each got their name, what each name means, and whether each was named after someone.

Many people believe that a person's name can influence future success because of the associations that the name has to other people and other factors that make an impression on others. For instance, someone with a name like Albert might be considered intelligent because of an association with the famous scientist Albert Einstein. Or someone with a name like Hope might leave a positive impression because of the meaning of the word *hope*. Do the names of the students in the DVD scenes here make any impression on you? If so, what? Discuss whether you think a person's name makes an immediate impression on others and how it can help or hinder one's ability to be successful? Give examples to support your view if possible.

Task 3

Can you and your partner list any short forms of the given names in Table 1? Do you have a nickname? If so, how did you get it? Which name do you prefer to be called by, your given name, your nickname, or your family name? Why?

Task 4

Even businesses and other institutions can have nicknames. Do you know the nicknames of McDonald's®, IBM®, and AT&T®? Can you think of any other businesses (global or local) that are known by a nickname?

Task 5

Find and interview someone you know that has a nickname and/or middle name. Find out how that person got his or her name(s).

One difficulty you may have is the pronunciation of family names. As you know, most family names in the United States originate in other countries, and this can be a source of uncertainty about how to pronounce them. To begin working on the pronunciation of family names, 30 of the most common surnames (family names) of people living in the United States in 1990 and 2000 are listed in Table 2.

TABLE 2. 30 Most Common American Surnames (U.S. Census 1990 and 2000)

1990			2000		
1. Smith	11. Anderson	21. Clark	1. Smith	11. Martinez	21. Lopez
2. Johnson	12. Thomas	22. Rodriguez	2. Johnson	12. Anderson	22. Lee
3. Williams	13. Jackson	23. Lewis	3. Williams	13. Taylor	23. Gonzalez
4. Jones	14. White	24. Lee	4. Brown	14. Thomas	24. Harris
5. Brown	15. Harris	25. Walker	5. Jones	15. Hernandez	25. Clark
6. Davis	16. Martin	26. Hall	6. Miller	16. Moore	26. Lewis
7. Miller	17. Thompson	27. Allen	7. Davis	17. Martin	27. Robinson
8. Wilson	18. Garcia	28. Young	8. Garcia	18. Jackson	28. Walker
9. Moore	19. Martinez	29. Hernandez	9. Rodriguez	19. Thompson	29. Perez
10. Taylor	20. Robinson	30. King	10. Wilson	20. White	30. Hall

Frequently Occurring Surnames from Census 2000, *www.census.gov/genealogy/www/freqnames2k.html*.
Accessed: June 23, 2008.
Frequently Occurring First Names and Surnames from the 1990 Census, *www.census.gov/genealogy/www/freqnames.html*.
Accessed: December 15, 2007.

Task 6

Look at Table 2, and identify any names that you are not sure how to pronounce. Can you and your partner guess anything about the possible country of origin of people with any of the 30 most common surnames? What changes do you notice from 1990 to 2000? What do you think is the most common surname in other countries, such as Mexico, Korea, Japan, Russia, or another country that you are familiar with?

Task 7

Are there any names of people that you interact with whose names you are not sure how to pronounce? Teachers? Office support staff? Colleagues? Make a short list, and then discuss the pronunciation of the names with a partner or partners. Ask your instructor for some help, if you need it.

Forms of Address

You may wonder sometimes how you should address your instructors (what to call them). Should you use a title only (e.g., Professor), a title plus family name (such as Professor Evans), or perhaps a first name? In some countries, the only choice may be to use the title and, optionally, the family name. While some instructors in the United States may also prefer that form of address, others may want you to be on a first-name basis with them (call them by their first name, like Jim). If you are not sure how to address your instructor, you can ask other students or the instructor. However, you would always be correct if you used a formal form of address such as Professor FAMILY NAME (Professor Evans) or Dr. FAMILY NAME (Dr. Evans).

Task 8

Ask three or four students who are not in your class how they address their instructors. Also ask these students about any confusion or uncertainty they may have had in relation to an instructor's name. Be prepared to report what you learn to your class. Here are a few questions to help you gather the information.

- How do you address your instructors? Do you use their titles and family name or something else?
- What form of address do you use for someone who is not a professor?
- Are you or have you ever been on a first name basis with any of your instructors? If yes, how did you know it was acceptable to use the instructor's first name?
- Are you comfortable using an instructor's first name? Why or why not?
- How are forms of address related to speaker status in the United States?

Names of Places

As you know, trying to figure out the correct pronunciation of someone's name can sometimes be difficult. The same is true for states, cities, streets, buildings, and other places. Even people who have lived in the United States for a long time may have questions about pronunciation. For example, visitors to Florida often want to pronounce the city of Kissimmee with the stress on the first syllable, while natives of the city place the stress on the second.

When it comes to names and places, the usual rules of pronunciation often do not apply for a variety of reasons. Some place names are derived from other languages but have been anglicized, as in Marseilles (mar-SAILS) in Illinois or Milan (MY-lun) in Michigan. Sometimes local tradition dictates how a name is pronounced. For instance, the town of Quincy in Massachusetts is pronounced "Quinzee" by locals and "Quinsee" by non-locals. Quincy in Illinois, on the other hand, is always "Quinsee." For local names, it may be best to ask someone who has some local knowledge.

Task 9

1. Some well-known U.S. cities are listed. With a partner, discuss how each one is pronounced. Pay particular attention to word stress. Mark those that you are not sure about.

Houston	Chicago	Phoenix
Albuquerque	Tucson	Indianapolis
Louisville	San Jose	Cincinnati
Philadelphia	Miami	Milwaukee

2. Bring a map of a U.S. state or Canadian province to class. If you are living in the U.S. or Canada, choose a map of your own state or province. With a partner, identify cities whose names you want to pronounce well enough to be understood. Work on the pronunciation.

3. It's important to both know where key buildings, structures, places, and streets on or near campus are and how to pronounce their names clearly. Work with a partner to create some lists of key buildings, streets, neighboring communities, and business establishments that you need to pronounce clearly. Work on your pronunciation of the items on the lists with the help of your instructor or someone else from your community.

What are some important buildings on your campus or in your community?

1. _____   3. _____

2. _____   4. _____

What are some main streets or roads? Consider also including the street where you live.

1. _____   3. _____

2. _____   4. _____

What are some neighboring cities and towns?

1. _____   3. _____

2. _____   4. _____

List some well-known businesses (including popular restaurants or stores).

1. _____   3. _____

2. _____   4. _____

Throughout the textbook, beginning with Task 10, we will frequently reference the Michigan Corpus of Academic Spoken English (MICASE).[1] The MICASE is a database of recordings made at the University of Michigan Ann Arbor campus. It contains 152 transcripts (1,848,364 words) of academic spoken English. Many of the transcripts we use have been modified or adapted for the purposes of the tasks. You can read the full transcripts and hear sound files of many of the transcripts at the website http://micase.umdl.umich.edu/m/micase/.

---

[1] R. C. Simpson, S. L. Briggs, J. Ovens, and J. M. Swales. (2002). *The Michigan Corpus of Academic Spoken English*. Ann Arbor: The Regents of the University of Michigan.

Locations and Directions

While it is often possible to get or give directions using the Internet, you still may need to verbally ask for or give directions. For instance, you may need to drop a paper off at your instructor's department or office in a building unfamiliar to you.

Task 10

This slightly edited discussion took place in an undergraduate history class at the end of the semester. Read through the interaction, and then discuss with a partner or partners the questions that follow. For ease of discussion, numbers have been added next to each turn.

1. **Instructor:** Will you return to class on Thursday?

2. **Student 1:** We'll be here.

3. **Student 2:** We'll be, we'll show up.

4. **Student 3:** Yeah dude we're, we're here all the time.

5. **Student 4:** We're like the core group.

6. **Student 2:** We're good students.

7. **Instructor:** You're the core group. There're another 50 people who never come, *<students laugh>*. Who never show up at all. And I appreciate having the group, the core group here. Um, so um, let me go let me go through the paper instructions with you.

8. **Student 3:** Do we get extra credit for coming? *<students laugh>* Like when you consider our grades? Keep in mind the core group who's here, on a regular basis?

9. **Instructor:** Well, I think that it'll show up in the grades. It's already shown up, in some of the stuff you've written and it'll show up, some more. Um . . . so, let's go through it again. Um, the paper is due in my mailbox at 4:00 PM on December 18th. Um, and then my mailbox is in University Towers, not Mason Hall. Okay? Is everyone okay with that?

10. **Student 4:** Can we drop it off at the history department?

11. **Instructor:** I would not do that, particularly at this time of year. Cuz the mail service is pretty bad.

12. **Student 4:** Cuz I don't know where University Towers is.

13. **Instructor:** Uh . . . the University Towers is the biggest building on South University Avenue.

14. **Student 4:** I guess I would have to know where South University is then, right? *<laugh>*

15. **Student 1:** It's by Ulrich's.

16. **Instructor:** South University starts at the Michigan Union and goes, heads east from there.

17. **Student 4:** Ulrich's.

18. **Student 2:** Ulrich's Cafe Ja- Cava Java.

19. **Student 1:** Jimmy John's.

20. **Instructor:** At the south end of the quad.

21. **Student 3:** Burger King.

22. **Student 1:** Brown Jug.

23. **Student 4:** Okay, okay *<students laugh>* I got that street.

24. **Student 1:** That's the street.

25. **Instructor:** Okay. There're two buildings . . .

26. **Student 1:** Right next door to Coney Town.

27. **Student 3:** Yeah, and like Hill is the cross street.

28. **Instructor:** Yeah mhm, two tall, two tall buildings—really tall buildings. The one is over here on Maynard . . . and the other one, University Towers is . . .

29. **Student 1:** South Forest.

30. **Student 3:** Forest. Forest. *<students laugh>*

31. **Instructor:** Okay, that's right.

32. **Student 1:** Yeah. South Forest. That's the cross street. South Forest and South University. It's on the corner.

33. **Instructor:** And the history department's on the second floor. And you can get into the building until five o'clock but, I'd like to have them by four. That's why I said four o'clock, so none of you have problems getting in.

(Based on MICASE. African History Lecture, File ID: LES315SU129)

> ### Notes
> - The Michigan Union is a building that all students at the University of Michigan know.
> - Ulrich's is a well-known campus bookstore.
> - The Brown Jug is a well-known campus restaurant.
> - Cava Java is a popular coffee shop.
> - Jimmy Johns® is a sandwich shop.
> - Coney Town is a restaurant.
> - South University, Hill, Maynard, and South Forest are major streets.

1. How would you describe the interaction between the students and the instructor in Turns 1 through 8? What does this part of the interaction reveal about the relationship between the students and the instructor? Would you feel comfortable engaging in this kind of talk with an instructor? Why or why not?

2. The instructor assumes all of the students know where South University is. What does Student 4 say to indicate that he/she does not know where this street is?

3. What kind of help do the students and the instructor give Student 4? Do they actually give directions?

4. How do you give directions? Do you use street names; directions that include north, south, east, and west; landmarks; or something else?

5. In which turn does Student 4 indicate that he/she knows where South University is? What does he/she say?

6. In Turn 27, Student 3 says, *Hill is the cross street,* and in Turn 32, Student 1 notes that the correct cross street is South Forest. What is a *cross street?*

7. Underline the expressions that describe a location. For instance, in Turn 20 the instructor says that Jimmy John's is *at the south end of the quad.*

8. What is a *quad*? Many campuses have quads but may use other terms to describe these spaces. For instance, Ohio State University has an Oval; Harvard University has a Yard; and the University of Michigan has a Diag as well as a Law Quad.

9. In Turn 28 the instructor says that one of the buildings is on *Maynard* and, in Turns 29 and 30, Students 1 and 3 don't let the instructor finish the sentence. Do you think this interruption was appropriate? Why or why not?

While it is possible to give explicit directions to a particular location, we have noticed in our analysis of the MICASE database that before giving any directions, it is very common to try to find out what locations the listener is familiar with. Thus, frequently a response to a request for directions will begin with a question, such as, *Do you know where . . . ?*

This interaction focuses on where an instructor's mailbox is. Notice how the instructor responds to the question with a question.

1. **Student 1:** Where is your mailbox by the way? I should probably ask—cuz the paper is due like in your mailbox on Tuesday.

2. **Instructor:** Oh yeah um it is um . . .Do you know where the door to our office is? I mean to our classroom is?

3. **Student 1:** Yeah.

4. **Instructor:** It is down three floors, and that same door. You see what I mean?

5. **Student 1:** Oh. Okay. On the first floor?

6. **Instructor:** Right. But the first door on your left as you, walk in . . . um, and uh the mail folders are on the left-hand side after you walk in the door, um and alphabetized. But um, it's a little confusing cuz there are two sets of folders. I don't know why *<student laughs>*, um so it's a little confusing. *<laugh>*

(Based on MICASE. Anthropology of American Cities Office Hours, File ID: OFC115SU060)

For more complicated directions and directions where there is no landmark that can be used, a speaker may orient you by telling you where you are and where you want to go, as demonstrated in the following task.

Task 11

Read the following interaction between a student at a Help Desk (Student 1) and a student looking for a room. The square brackets indicate overlapping speech. With a partner, complete the tasks that follow the transcript.

1. **Student 1:** Can I help you? Hi.
2. **Student 2:** Yes, I'm looking for room sixteen.
3. **Student 1:** Okay, We're at the central desk and all the rooms are behind us, kind of.
4. **Student 2:** Okay, I only found up to fifteen. *<laugh>*
5. **Student 1:** Okay. If you go straight [**Student 2:** Uhuh] and make a right around the corner [**Student 2:** Uhuh] You want to go through the double doors and pass the copy room, and it'll be on your right-hand side. You pass it, go around the corner make a left. It's right next to the elevator.
6. **Student 2:** Okay.
7. **Student 1:** It's kind of, *<points>* so you're going straight. [**Student 2:** Mmkay] You're making a right. [**Student 2:** Right] And then, make a left around the corner. [**Student 2:** Okay] You'll get there.
8. **Student 2:** Okay, thank you.
9. **Student 1:** Sure.

(Based on MICASE. Media Union Service Encounters, File ID: SVC999MX104)

1. In Turn 2 the student says, *I'm looking for room sixteen.* What other expressions could he/she have used to ask for directions to Room 16? Write as many as you can.

   _____

   _____

   _____

2. Student 2 does a very good job of giving feedback to indicate that he/she is following the directions. Write the expressions he/she uses to accomplish this.

   _____

   _____

   _____

3. What verbs does Student 1 use to direct Student 2 to the room? Which of these verb phrases would work as well?

take a right	*walk left*	*go right*
turn left	*hang a right*	*stay left / stay to your left*

4. List the prepositional phrases that Student 1 uses to identify a location (for instance, the rooms are *on the first floor*).

5. Here are some other common expressions indicating a location. The prepositions have been omitted. Choose a preposition that can complete each expression.
   a. The Modern Language Building is _____ the corner of Thayer and Washington Streets.
   b. The International Center is _____ State and Madison Streets.
   c. The Science Library is _____ the Dow Building _____ Hubbard Road.
   d. The lecture hall is _____ the 4th floor.
   e. Our classroom is _____ the end of the hallway.

6. In Turn 5 Student 1 says, *You want to go through the double doors and pass the copy room.* Can you think of another expression that could have been used besides *you want to go*?

7. How does Student 1 respond when Student 2 says *thank you* in Turn 8? What other responses are possible in this turn?

8. Now, look at a map of your town or campus. Describe for your partner the locations of a library and/or health service facility (clinic or hospital). Your partner will describe where to find a post office and a theater or performing arts center.

Task 12

Describe for a partner the location of a favorite restaurant, store, coffee shop, or other place that your partner is unfamiliar with. Also describe for your partner how to get from your current classroom to another classroom.

DVD Task

Unit 1: Places and Directions
Scenes 1–5

In these scenes, students are giving directions or describing a location in response to a question asked by another student.

Working in pairs, give your partner directions to your favorite local restaurant, your favorite place to hang out with friends, your next class, or your instructor's campus mailbox. Use your classroom as your starting point.

A response to a request for directions or locations may at times involve a lot of body language, such as pointing or turning in the direction of the destination. In fact, sometimes the non-verbal clues alone may be sufficient. For example, for simple directions a speaker may say things like, *It's right over there* and then point or turn toward the direction. Speakers may also use *up* and *down* to indicate direction. The choice of *up* and *down* depends on the orientation of the speaker. *Up* usually refers to away from the direction of the speaker's orientation to the listener, while *down* could be away and in the opposite direction. Read through these short interactions, and note the use of *up* and *down*.

INTERACTION 1

1. **Student 1:** Do you know if there's a directory for this building? I'm looking for a guy named Gary uh um Gary Hecker in the in um in the Advising Office.

2. **Student 2:** Yeah, uh Gary Hecker? Down this hall and then right at the next hallway. First door on the left.

3. **Student 1:** Okay, thanks.

INTERACTION 2

1. **Student 1:** Excuse me, uh uh can you tell me where Parking Services is?

2. **Student 2:** Um on Thompson. Yeah um just up Division to Jefferson. Then right, uh no no left. [**Student 1:** Left mhmm okay] Keep going till Thompson. It should be on the right near the parking lot.

3. **Student 1:** Okay, up to Jefferson and left to Thompson and then right, I got it.

Ellipsis

You have probably noticed that in many of the interactions you have looked at so far, speakers do not use complete sentences, or sentences that follow the rules of grammar that you might have learned. Read this interaction between two students doing a biology lab that involved bird watching, and underline the sentences that seem to be missing grammatical elements.

1. **Student 1:** I see a bird. I see an American Goldfinch.

2. **Student 2:** Where?

3. **Student 1:** Down there. In that bush over there.

4. **Student 2:** Where?

5. **Student 1:** The taller one, the closest. See the um, that that dead branch?

6. **Student 2:** That branch up there? Yeah I see it. To the left of it? I was looking at that bird, but I couldn't. . . I didn't know what that was.

7. **Student 1:** There were like ten of those in there and they all just flew up and then went down.

8. **Student 2:** Okay.

(Based on MICASE. Biology of Birds Field Lab, File ID: LAB175SU026)

Ellipsis is the term used to describe the omission of a portion of a phrase or a sentence. The word *ellipsis* comes from Greek, meaning "falling short." This makes sense because ellipsis involves leaving out words or phrases.

Ellipsis is a difficult aspect of language to master. Often, new learners of English do not use much ellipsis while speaking because it seems to break many perceived rules of how the language works. When a speaker does not include ellipsis in his or her speech, however, it often makes the language sound a bit stilted (formal). Also, if you are not aware of ellipsis, you may constantly be thinking that you are missing something and have serious listening comprehension problems. Here we provide only a quick look at ellipsis. Unit 5 provides a more thorough discussion.

Task 13

To get some sense of what elements are omitted in speech, try to identify the missing elements in the bird watching example. Can you rewrite it to create turns consisting of complete sentences? For example, if we look at Turn 2 in the transcript on page 16, we see that the subject and verb are missing. If we rewrite so that the sentence has all the usual grammatical elements, we can write, *where is it?*

1. **Student 1:** I see a bird. I see an American Goldfinch.

2. **Student 2:** Where?

   Missing elements: <u>Subject and verb.</u>

   Full form: <u>Where is it?</u>

3. **Student 1:** Down there. In that bush over there.

   Missing elements: _____

   Full form: _____

4. **Student 2:** Where?

   Missing elements: _____

   Full form: _____

5. **Student 1:** The taller one, the closest. See the um, that that dead branch?

   Missing elements: _____

   Full form: _____

6. **Student 2:** That branch up there? Yeah I see it. To the left of it? I was looking at that bird, but I couldn't . . . I didn't know what that was.

   Missing elements: _____

   Full form: _____

Consider the structure of a grammatical sentence in English. In each of these examples, some part of the sentence is missing. Why is this part of the sentence not necessary?

Naming Places and Things after Famous People

As you walk or drive around your campus or community, you might have noticed that many streets and buildings are clearly named after someone or something. For instance, many professional sports venues are named after a product brand or company: Comerica Park in Detroit, U.S. Cellular Field and Wrigley Field in Chicago, or Busch Stadium in St. Louis (the latter two also happen to be the family names of the company founders). Airports are often named for an important (or at least important at one time) public figure, as in LaGuardia Airport in New York and Lindbergh Field in San Diego. Streets and highways may be named for a prominent settler of a region or a person who made a significant contribution to a city or even a country, as in La Salle Avenue (in San Francisco), which was named after Robert Cavelier de la Salle, a French explorer. Buildings, too, are often named after people. On university, college, and community college campuses, it is common to name a building after a person who made a significant intellectual or monetary contribution to the institution. For example, Cornell University has Rockefeller Hall named for John M. Rockefeller, who gave the money to build it. Unfortunately, sometimes the significance of the people for whom a building is named may not be clear today.

Task 14

This is the first of several group presentation projects in this textbook. For this first project you have two options. Use the form on page 19 to help you and your partner(s) get organized. Together decide what information each of you will gather and how you will gather it. To maximize your speaking practice, it is a good idea to interview at least one person who has information that you need. You can also collect information by making phone calls, finding information on the Internet, or visiting places to pick up printed information or observe what happens there.

After you collect the information, decide together how you will present it to the class or to a small group in class, whichever your instructor prefers. Each presenter should be prepared to speak for two minutes and then answer questions. Two minutes is not a lot of time; you should practice your presentation several times so you can deliver the information without reading it.

OPTION A

With a partner (or partners) choose a building or facility on your campus or in your town that is named after someone or something, as in the examples. Find some information on how and why the name was chosen. You should include information on the location as well as the significance of the person your chosen building or facility is named after. Discuss interesting features of the structure as well. If possible, using your classroom as a starting point, give directions to the building or facility you have chosen.

Group Presentation:
Finding Out about Buildings, Facilities, or Other Places around Town or Campus

Building, facility, or place: _____

Group Members	Presentation Responsibilities

Main message: _____

Do you think you should use a visual? If yes, what kind? _____

OPTION B

Choose one of the subjects listed that you would like to investigate to help your classmates learn more about the community where you live or attend school. For each topic, think about the kind of information that would be interesting to your class. Consider such things as location, prices, hours of operation, and any special features. We have included a few questions you may want to consider for each topic.

1. **Restaurants.** Find information about three popular places to eat. What is each restaurant known for? Which of the restaurants would others recommend? How much should you tip?

2. **Pizza places.** Find information about three pizza places. Do they deliver? How long does delivery usually take? Should you tip the delivery person?

3. **Food shopping.** Find information about three good places to buy food. How do these places differ? Which has the best quality? Which is most convenient for students?

4. **Parks.** Find information about three popular parks. What special activities can you do there? Do the parks sponsor any special events?

5. **Movie theaters.** Find information about three places to watch movies. Are there any unique features about the movie theaters? Are there any student discounts?

6. **Bookstores.** Find information about three bookstores. What kinds of books and other products can you buy there? Do they hold special events there?

7. **Cafés.** Find information about three cafés near campus. What kind of food can you buy at these cafés? Can you get free wireless Internet access there?

8. **Music.** Find information about three popular places to listen to music. Is there a charge to get in? Will you be carded?[2] Can people dance? What kind of people go there?

---

[2] *To be carded* means you are asked for identification to prove you are old enough to buy alcoholic beverages.

Pronunciation Focus: Sentence Stress

Introduction

In English, rhythm and stress go hand in hand. When speaking, content words—nouns, verbs, adjectives, and adverbs—are usually stressed. The remaining words (such as prepositions and articles) in a sentence are usually not emphasized and may be linked to surrounding words. In these sentences, which words are content words that should be emphasized? Which words do you think would likely not be stressed?

1. I had an exam last night.
2. My project is due next week.
3. The review session is tomorrow at 8:00.
4. The mailboxes are on the fourth floor.

Data Collection and Analysis

Part 1: Transcription

With one or two partners listen to either Unit 1, Names, Scene 1, 2, or 3 on the DVD, and then choose one to two minutes of speech to transcribe. Each of you should transcribe what you hear, listening to the DVD as many times as you need. You can listen together or individually. Once everyone is done transcribing, compare your transcriptions and try to create a complete transcript of the section you chose. Listen to the DVD again if necessary. Indicate any places in the recording where you cannot figure out what is being said and ask your instructor for some assistance.

Part 2: Analysis

With your partners, mark the content words that are stressed as well as the pauses. Write your observations on sentence stress.

Part 3: Report to the class

Your report should provide the following information:

1. Remind your listeners of the focus of your investigation.
2. What, if anything, made it difficult to identify the sentence stress? Was it the vocabulary or grammar? The recording? The speakers' rates of speaking? Characteristics of the speakers' pronunciations?
3. What are your group's observations on sentence stress? What, if any, other interesting pronunciation observations did your group make?

Part 4: Production

With a partner, read aloud and/or role-play your transcript, paying special attention to the content words and sentence stress.

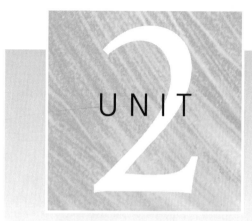

U N I T

2

Academic Life: Student and Instructor Roles

In his article, "Getting the Most out of the U.S. Higher Education Experience: An Inside Perspective," Edward Bodine (2005) states that "for international students, who may be used to a different institutional culture and social organization at their home universities, American campus life may seem to them strange, perplexing, and no doubt a little overwhelming, especially at the start of the school year." For any new student, adjustment to life on campus can be both a frustrating and rewarding experience.

Unit 2 focuses on the daily lives of students and their instructors. It primarily concerns student-instructor behavior in the classroom and expectations instructors have of their students. It also deals with attitudes students have toward their instructors and class work.

By the end of the unit, you should be able to

- share cultural differences you have experienced in your classroom
- understand some common idiomatic expressions used by instructors and students
- design and conduct an interview to gather information to present to your class or group
- make a short presentation that summarizes information you have collected.

The Student Experience

The student experience in a North American academic environment can be as varied as individual students. However, students everywhere deal with quite similar concerns when adjusting to a new academic environment. To get accustomed to a new environment, students often turn to other students and learn from their experiences. Task 1 presents an interview of a student giving advice to other students who will be studying in the United States.

Task 1

In this interview, Apratim Sahay, an undergraduate student from India,[1] discusses his experiences during his first year at the University of Chicago and gives some advice to other Indians planning to study in the United States. As you read the interview, think about your own experiences in a different academic environment and how you would describe them. With your partner or group, discuss the questions that follow.

What are classes really like?

> In one word: Fun. In two: Serious fun. Professors and students are genuinely interested in what they are doing. Most humanities and core classes are small (about 20) and discussion-oriented, which is a big change from the note-taking back in India. The classes here, especially in math and science, are going to take a lot out of you. New concepts will hit you at an extremely fast pace. All the groundwork they have been laying about this being a rigorous school, life of the mind blah-blah is for real. . . .

What are the professors really like?

> All of them are incredibly smart. They are going to be some of the most frighteningly smart people you've ever met, the kinds with 3 Ph.D.s even in subjects they aren't teaching. They are going to continuously challenge you, at the same time they are extremely approachable (although intimidating) during office hours. Professors here are quite frankly a breed of their own, they are unique, and yes, crazy about their work . . . My physics prof is this goofy British guy who keeps doing weird stuff in class. He sat on a wheelchair today along with this fire extinguisher thing in this hand, then turned it on and went whizzing in the opposite direction! And we went on to derive the equations for rocket propulsion after that!

---

[1] University of Chicago Prospective Students Advisory Committee (PSAC)'s International Student Profiles, http://psac.uchicago.edu/profiles/tim.html.

What do you do for fun?

I play squash, table tennis (ping pong here), and tennis. The Ratner Athletic Center . . . [has] awesome workout facilities, and a huge Olympic-size swimming pool. For this quarter, I'm not involved with any clubs and other activities because I have enough on my plate right now. But getting involved with the SASA (South Asian Student Association) and the newspapers is on my list for later.

What challenges have you faced here? Were there things that were difficult to adjust to?

Food. Food. Food. American food tastes like nothing you've tasted before. Think McDonalds and Pizza Hut. Think burgers and fries and pizzas 24/7, each day, every meal. . . . Think salads . . . that yucky green stuff that your mom forced you to eat. . . . You know that 64 kgs that you are allowed to bring, load it with food, masalas, achars, whatever you can find. Learn cooking from your mom. . . . And come prepared to be homesick. I missed home like nothing ever, trust me there will be times when you will be literally dying to speak Hindi. . . .

How cold is it really?

It gets cold, really really cold. It's the kind of cold that will make you wish that you had never been born, or if you are a clearer thinker, wish you had never come here. -20C is what it's going to be like. It's going to be so cold that your nose hairs will freeze, the coffee in your hand will freeze, polar bears will die. . . . Actually don't even try to imagine the cold. It's impossible; we in India can't fathom it. . . . But people survive; you will too. . . .

1. Does it appear that Apratim is adjusting well to university life in Chicago? Why or why not?

2. What clues does Apratim give you about what type of school he attends? What kind of student do you think he is?

3. Apratim refers to his professor as *this goofy British guy who keeps doing weird stuff in class.* What's his opinion of this professor? How can you tell? What does *goofy* and *weird stuff* mean?

4. Give a couple of examples of how this student exaggerates to make a point.

5. This student uses a lot of interesting expressions. Explain the expressions in italics.
   - life of the mind *blah-blah* is for real
   - Think burgers and fries and pizzas *24/7*
   - Think salads . . . that *yucky green stuff* your mom forced you to eat
   - I'm not involved with any clubs and other activities because *I have enough on my plate* right now.
   - The Ratner Athletic Center here has *awesome workout facilities.*
   - And don't even try to imagine the cold. . . . *We in India can't fathom it.*

Task 2

Working in pairs or in a group, discuss how your answers to the interview questions would be similar or different from Apratim's. Relate some of your experiences adjusting to your current academic environment.

What are classes like?

What are your instructors like?

What do you do for fun?

What challenges have you faced here?

What was the most significant adjustment you had to make?

What advice would you give to a student from another country who is planning to study in a North American college or university? The following expressions using *would* are useful:

I would tell someone that they[2]. . . .

I would tell them to . . . .

It would be good to . . . .

My advice would be to . . . .

Notice how the word *would* is used in this hypothetical situation to convey advice.[3] The language for giving advice and suggestions is covered in more detail in Unit 4.

DVD Task

Unit 2: Student Life

Scenes 1–2

In these scenes, students are talking about some of the ways they have had to adjust to life at a U.S. university. In Scene 1, an international student is talking about some differences between the United States and his home country; in Scene 2, a new American student is talking about his first year living in a dormitory.

In these scenes, what active listening strategies does each of the listeners use to provide feedback to the speaker and keep the conversation going? What differences do you notice?

---

[2] In conversational English, instead of referring to someone as *he* or *she*, it is common to use the plural *they*.

[3] A subordinate *if* clause can precede the main clause in these hypothetical situations, such as, *If I were going to give some advice to new students, I would tell them that they should keep up with their homework.*

Interviewing and Communicating What You Learn

Question-asking is a common feature of many interactions both in and out of the academic community. As someone new to an academic culture, being comfortable asking questions to get information can help you adjust more quickly to your surroundings. It can also help you establish and maintain friendships or participate in social interactions. Let's begin with an easy exercise that gives some practice asking questions.

Task 3

This task has two parts. First, on a piece of paper, write four statements about yourself, one of which must be false. Do not indicate which statement is false. Then exchange papers with a classmate.

Second, read the statements your classmate has written. Take a moment, and write at least four questions you will ask your classmate in order to find out more about him/her and to help you determine which statement is false. When you are ready, ask each other your questions. Ask more questions if you need to in order to decide which statement is false. Did you guess correctly?

In addition to asking questions in social interactions or in informal classroom situations such as in Task 3, you may have to ask questions in more formal, structured interviews as a means of gathering information for a course presentation or paper. To increase your confidence in conducting interviews, we will look at the steps of a simple structured interview. After learning about the interview process, you will have several opportunities to conduct your own interviews with other students, instructors, and service personnel in your own academic community.

We have divided the interview process into these five steps.

1. Choosing the focus of your interview and deciding what questions to ask.
2. Finding a suitable interviewee and requesting an interview.
3. Conducting the interview.
4. Choosing and summarizing relevant information you gathered from the interviewee.
5. Presenting the summary of the information you gathered to an audience.

Let's look at the steps in more detail.

STEP 1: CHOOSING A FOCUS AND DECIDING WHAT QUESTIONS TO ASK

Before coming up with questions, you need to decide what kind of information you want, and then determine your focus. If you have a clear focus, you should be able to get specific information in a relatively short amount of time. After you have decided a focus, come up with the specific questions you want to ask. Avoid asking broad questions such as *Tell me about your experiences here so far.* Instead request more specific information, such as *Tell me about your experience on your first day of classes* or *Was your first day of classes what you expected?* Asking very specific questions such as these can also lead to some interesting discussion.

Preceding Interview Questions with a Statement

Some interviewers make a statement before they ask a question. Look at these examples.

1. Some new students begin to get involved in activities and clubs when they first come to campus. What activities have you taken part in or what groups have you joined since you got here?
2. Some students have said that professors here are quite accessible to students. How would you characterize one or two of your professors?
3. New students sometimes have trouble organizing their time during their first semester. What strategies would you recommend?

Asking Follow-Up Questions

After you have prepared and organized a list of questions to ask your interviewee, you may worry that the interview will seem somewhat rigid or unnatural. One way to make it more natural is to ask follow-up questions based on the interviewee's answers to your initial questions. Follow-up questions allow you to delve further into the topic with the interviewee. Some follow-up questions can be prepared before the interview; others, however, are best formulated more spontaneously in response to the interviewee's answer to the initial question. These require concentration and quick thinking on the part of the interviewer. As the interview goes on, you may find yourself becoming less tied to your original questions as you modify your initial interview plan.

Task 4

Let's look at the sequence of question–response–follow-up question. In the following situations, what follow-up question would you ask given the interviewee's response? An example is provided for you.

Example

Question: Do you think it's easy to make friends on campus?

Response: I've been lucky because I met some nice people during my first semester on campus.

Follow-up question: *That's great. Where did you meet them? In class?*

1. Question: When you first became a university/college student, what was the hardest thing to get used to?

   Response: My roommate stayed up later than me and wanted to keep the light on.

   Follow-up question: _____

2. Question: Can you give me an idea of what one of your instructors is like?

Response: My art instructor seems rather informal. He wears blue jeans to class. We're supposed to call him by his first name.

Follow-up question: _____

3. Question: Do you just study or do you also have a job?

Response: I work and study.

Follow-up question: _____

4. Question: What was your first day of classes like?

Response: It was really embarrassing. I missed my first class because I got on the wrong bus.

Follow-up question: _____

STEP 2: FINDING AN INTERVIEWEE AND REQUESTING AN INTERVIEW

Finding an interviewee may be fairly easy if you decide to interview a classmate, roommate, or co-worker. However, if you decide to approach someone that you don't know, say, in one of your classes or in a café, what would you initially say to the person? How would you make a request for an interview?

Task 5

Look at this introduction. What purpose does each section serve?

	Purpose
Hi. My name is Adam.	
I'm a first-year student at the university	
and I'm doing an interview on campus life for one of my classes.	
Would you have a couple of minutes to answer some questions for me?	

Making a Request

Notice that the speaker used a simple request: *Would you have a couple of minutes to answer some questions for me?* The language of requests will be discussed in detail in Unit 3. For now, here are several other ways you could make a polite request for an interview.

1. I was wondering if you could answer a couple of questions for me about some experiences and impressions you had as a first-year student.

2. Could I ask you a few questions about your first semester on campus?

3. Would it be okay for me to ask you a few questions about being a student in the music school?

STEP 3: CONDUCTING THE INTERVIEW

Starting, Greetings, Thanks

If you set up your interview at a separate time from the initial request, it is typical to start the interview with a greeting and to thank the person for agreeing to the interview. Look at these examples.

Hi, I'm Erin.   Thanks for agreeing to the interview.

Thanks for letting me interview you.

Thanks for taking time for this interview today.

Ending the Interview

It is important to be considerate of the interviewee's time, especially if you do not know the person you are interviewing. If the interviewee doesn't have much time or time is running out, one strategy is to select your most interesting questions and eliminate the others. You can also let your interviewee know that you are almost done. There are a number of ways to end an interview. What strategies did these speakers use?

1. Well, thanks for taking time to talk to me. It was interesting hearing about some of the experiences you had during your first semester. It sounds like you really like being a student. Good luck with your studies.

2. Well, I think those are all the questions I have. Thanks for the information. I really appreciate it. It was nice talking to you.

3. You said you had to leave for class at 1:00 so I guess we'll stop here. It's been really useful hearing about how you juggle work and studies. Thanks a lot for the interview.

STEPS 4 AND 5: SUMMARIZING AND PRESENTING THE INFORMATION

After conducting your interview, decide which information you would like to include for an informal presentation for your partner, group, or class. Prepare a summary, and decide on the organizational structure that best suits your information. For example, you may wish to narrate a story the interviewee told you using chronological order. Or you may want to group information by topic, for example information about school, work, or sports. You could also use enumeration to list points made by the person you interviewed (e.g., strategies the interviewee recommends for making friends or studying for exams). Finally, you could use comparison and contrast to discuss, for example, how your experiences differ from those of the interviewee.

Task 6

Interview a student from one of your other classes to find out about his or her experiences as a first-semester undergraduate or graduate student. First, prepare a series of questions (including follow-ups) aimed at finding out about the interviewee's experiences and observations as a new student. Follow the steps outlined for conducting an interview. After you collect the information, prepare a presentation for your classmates.

Students and Instructors in the Classroom

As a new student, you may find it challenging to adapt to the classroom environment. You may be confused about what is considered acceptable student behavior, what expectations instructors have of their students, and how to respond to your instructor's teaching style.

Task 7

In small groups, use this questionnaire to discuss your classroom experiences so far. How does this differ from your prior academic experience?

Questions for Discussion	Observations: Current Academic Situation	Observations: Prior Academic Experience
1. What do students and instructors wear to class?		
2. What things—besides the typical notebooks, pens, and pencils—do students bring with them to class?		
3. What teaching style do instructors generally use?		
4. Do instructors usually come prepared for class?		
5. Do students generally come prepared for class?		
6. In class, how do students act toward their instructors? Do you think they show respect? Explain.		
7. What kind of homework assignments do the instructors give? How would you describe the workload?		
8. How do students interact with each other inside the class?		

1. What surprised you the most about the students' and instructors' behaviors?

2. What differences in classroom behavior have been the hardest for you to adjust to?

Share some of your group's findings with the class.

Task 8

Interview any new international student to find out about his or her classroom experience. Use some of the questions for discussion in Task 7. If you like, include a few of your own questions.

Compile the information from your interview. Prepare an oral and/or written summary of your findings to share with a small group or the entire class.

The Instructor Experience

Just as every student has unique experiences in the academic community, so do instructors. While you usually get to know your instructors in a specific context, that of the classroom, there are other aspects to their academic lives that you may not know much about. Learning more about the daily lives of instructors may help you gain some insights into their professional lives and also help you interact more successfully with them.

Task 9

With your partner or group discuss this question: What are some job-related responsibilities or activities you think your instructors have outside of class?

Most students meet professors in class or for office hours. Some professors also meet their students more informally for coffee or invite them to their homes. But many students may not know exactly what their professors do all day, especially what kinds of non-teaching responsibilities they have.

Task 10

This excerpt is from a series of presentations sponsored by the Career Planning and Placement Office at the University of Michigan. The presentation was given by a professor in electrical engineering and computer science. He is talking to a group of students who are considering an academic career. The professor works with ten Master's and PhD students. He is married and has three children. In this talk he describes his typical teaching and non-teaching days. This is his description of the non-teaching day. After reading it, answer the questions that follow. Sentence numbers have been added for ease of discussion.

(1) I decided potentially the best thing to do is to give you a snapshot of my daily life. Um what do I do during the day? . . . (2) I took yesterday as a representative day (Monday, twenty-second of February) this is what my day looked like. (3) Um at nine o'clock every Monday morning I have a research group meeting. (4) Uh, that's actually at central campus interestingly enough, not on North Campus. (5) That lasts till ten-thirty. (6) Right after that I rush to my office, answer e-mail, put out a few fires and and in this case I had a few minutes left and I wrote a bunch of reference letters that were pending, um and attempted to do that. (7) I had about forty-five minutes. (8) Got that done and then I had allocated myself an hour to finish editing this journal article that we've been working on and trying to put some finishing touches on it. (9) And sure enough at noon right before I had to go to my my lunch meeting I realized that I wasn't done and I had more stuff to do. (10) But there's no time left during the day.

(11) Probably the most enjoyable part of it (the day) was I had a lunch meeting, which I usually uh, almost every day of the week I have lunch meetings and often it's with my graduate students uh who are in my research group two or three of them at a time that

are working on a project. (12) Right after that I had a review of a defense talk by one of my graduate students who's going to do her defense in a couple of weeks. (13) After that I have about an hour that I have a T.A. (teaching assistant) meeting, as well as I do uh course preparation for my lecture on Tuesday.

(14) Um right after that there's a software seminar that we run every Monday and usually during this time of year we have faculty candidates come through. (15) I went and attended that. (16) The reason for that is because I had to have dinner with the faculty candidate (so) I had to attend the talk, at least. (17) Um I also serve on the search committee so it was important to do that. (18) Uh, I had fifteen twenty minutes right after that. (19) I answered a few phone calls and answered, uh, my email. (20) At five to six I had another research meeting with a couple of my graduate students, and then around six fifteen, I rushed and had dinner with our department head and uh our faculty candidate who was visiting. (21) My wife had just returned from out of town and I had forgotten to tell her, uh that I was having dinner with this faculty guy and uh I got on the phone and called her up and I said uh I think I mentioned this to you but I may have forgotten, and she said yep you sure did, and that was the end of that.

(22) Usually that's what my day looks like. (23) I have a bunch of Rs and Ws (in my schedule). (24) Late at night I tend to do a lot of reading, a lot of writing, some more reading some more writing. (25) But R also stands for relaxing and W also stands for watching television. (26) So it's a it's a combination of various things.

(Based on MICASE. Career Planning and Placement Workshop File ID: COL999MG053)

1. What's your reaction to this professor's account of his typical day? Does anything surprise you?

2. On his non-teaching day, what types of contact does he have with students? His colleagues?

3. In Sentence 1, what does the professor mean by a *snapshot* of his daily life?

4. In Sentence 6, the professor says, *I rush to my office, answer email, put out a few fires.* What's another way of saying *put out a few fires?*

5. In Sentence 6, the professor refers to a *bunch* of reference letters and in Sentence 9, he talks about having more *stuff* to do. What do *bunch* and *stuff* mean? Is this academic English? Check MICASE to see how common these expressions are.

6. In Sentence 6, the professor begins by using the present tense and ends by using the past tense. Why?

7. What does *Got that done* mean in Sentence 8? This is an example of ellipsis. What word has been eliminated, and why is it possible to eliminate it? (Further discussion of ellipsis can be found in Units 1 and 5.)

8. The professor uses the time expression *right after that* in Sentences 6, 12, and 14. Why does he use that particular expression?

9. What does the professor mean when he says faculty candidates *come through* in Sentence 14? Why do they *come through*? In Sentence 15, the professor says *I went and attended that*. What does *that* refer to?

10. In Sentence 21, the professor discusses a telephone call he makes to his wife. What's the purpose of the call? What does he say to her, and what is her response?

11. The professor discusses *Rs and Ws* in his schedule. What does it tell you about the professor's home life?

12. Finally, how does the professor organize his presentation?

This description is just one example of a "typical" non-teaching day. For other instructors, this might not be typical at all. Task 11 gives you the opportunity to find out more about typical days of one of your instructors.

DVD Task

Unit 2: An Instructor's Day
Scene 1

In this scene, a professor and a teaching assistant (TA) from the same department are talking about the challenges of their jobs as instructors.

Watch the DVD, and then identify all the non-teaching responsibilities the instructor and the teaching assistant have. Do any of these surprise you? Discuss. What do you think are some of the advantages and disadvantages of being a teaching assistant?

Task 11

Interview one of your instructors from another class to find out how a typical day unfolds. Before the interview, be sure to prepare a few focused questions to ask. After the interview, reflect on what you learned. In what ways was this instructor's day similar to and different from the professor's in Task 10? Present what you learn to a small group of your classmates.

Instructor Expectations Regarding Email from Students

On his non-teaching days, the engineering professor you read about in Task 10 spends time both in the morning and afternoon answering his email. Some messages may be from colleagues and administrators. Others may be personal. But a portion of the email is likely from students. Instructors may have specific expectations of how email correspondence is to be used in their course. If so, they usually make these expectations known in the class syllabus or verbally during class.

Task 12

In these excerpts from six different classroom sessions, the instructors bring up the topic of email and their expectations about when students should email them. With your partner, read the first three questions, and look for the answers as you read the excerpts. Then continue with the questions on page 37.

1. In what circumstances do these instructors suggest students email them?

2. What alternatives to email does the instructor suggest in Excerpt 1?

3. What limitations do professors place on emailing in Excerpts 3 and 4? Explain.

EXCERPT 1

Instructor: Homework number one is a math review. For most of you this will be a review . . . , will take ten minutes and you'll be done. But if you have questions about that, chapter one is a good reference. I have office hours on Monday and I have email and I'm very good about answering email. So, if you're intimidated by that, don't be. We just wanna make sure we all start out understanding the difference between a meter and a centimeter. . . .

(Based on MICASE. Intro Astronomy Discussion Section, File ID: DIS150JU130)

EXCERPT 2

Instructor: I'm also covering the course materials based on the feedback I get from you. It is important before we discuss topics, that you email me, with questions that you have on that particular topic so that I can maybe address them here in the lecture. Okay as best I can. Or I will tell you that it is not going to be addressed in the lecture because you are to discover that in the lab, and it will be discussed in your discussion.

(Based on MICASE. Inorganic Chemistry Lecture, File ID: LEL200JU105)

EXCERPT 3

Instructor: Um, I tend to look at email first thing in the morning, and last thing at night, so if you have sent me a message, um, I will give you a relatively full answer I will do that for you. But, um you might wanna check, you know last thing Wednesday night . . . or . . . first thing Thursday morning. Now, what I, what I will not respond to is how should I answer X. That I won't respond to but if you have a thought to offer. . . . I would respond to your ideas and tell you what I thought either of the idea itself, or of the evidence, or or of the presentation.

(Based on MICASE. History Review Discussion Section, File ID: DIS315JU101)

EXCERPT 4

Instructor: First um I don't want you to rely on me to give you the assignment if you're absent from class. . . . So what I suggest is that you get a buddy so if you miss class and want to find out if there was a writing assignment, then I suggest you not email me, much less call me, but email your buddy.

(Based on MICASE. American Literature Lecture, File ID: LES300SU103)

EXCERPT 5

Instructor: I have office hours on Monday right after the lecture. How many people have class then? Okay, about half of you. So for half of you that's not a convenient time, for the other half, it's just, take the elevator up to the ninth floor and visit. For those of you who can't meet during that time, just email me and I'll set up another time to meet with you. . . . So not a problem. Also if you have a question that you don't really need to set up an office hour like is this a good start to an answer for number three? Just email me and I'll try to get back to you within a day. So if there are less complicated things, that's an easier way to ask questions.

(Based on MICASE. Intro Astronomy Discussion Section, File ID: DIS150JU130)

EXCERPT 6

Instructor: If you wanna come talk to me about papers, just email me and then, I I mean emailing me first and saying like I wanna come talk to you about the paper, sets me up, to kind of know like, what you wanna ask me about.

(Based on MICASE. Graduate French Cinema Seminar, File ID: SEM545MG083)

1. In Excerpt 1, what does the instructor mean by *that* when he says *if you're intimidated by that, don't be?*

2. In Excerpt 4, what does the instructor mean by *I suggest you not email me, much less call me?*

3. In Excerpt 4, what is a *buddy?*

Unit 3 provides more detail on emailing instructors.

Student Attitudes toward Homework

I won't accept late homeworks unless you're near death, or have a valid excuse that's of equal magnitude.

(From MICASE. University of Michigan Instructor, Intro Astronomy Discussion Section, File ID: DIS150JU130)

Homework is a major part of academic life. The amount and type of homework you have may vary widely depending on your degree program and the type of courses you are taking. Both instructors and students also vary greatly in their attitudes toward homework. Some instructors will insist that homework be handed in on time, while others may be more flexible. Some students may be highly organized, plan ahead, finish before deadlines. Others may procrastinate, putting off homework until the last minute. Many students fall somewhere in between these two extremes.

Task 13

With your partner or group, talk about the amount of homework you get in your classes. Did you expect the amount you are getting? How do you handle your homework? In other words, what strategies do you use for getting your homework done? What advice would you give a new student?

It is common for students to tell homework-related stories. Sometimes the stories are meant to amuse, and sometimes they are simply a way to complain. And sometimes students need to explain to their instructors why homework did not get done.

Task 14

In these excerpts, students tell stories related to their homework. The students in the second excerpt are junior and senior undergraduates. Read the stories, and then discuss the questions that follow.

EXCERPT 1

Student: When I was a law student, I worked full time and went to school at night. I'd have to do all my homework for the next week on the weekend. So, on Friday I'd hit the books and study till Sunday night, with a few breaks here and there like sometimes I'd go to the movies. I read almost everything I was assigned but by Wednesday or Thursday I couldn't remember some of the stuff I'd read. It took me four years to get through. I got good grades cuz I reviewed a lot for the exams. But I was a wreck when I graduated.

EXCERPT 2 (Statistics Office Hours)

1. **Instructor:** So you told me why you didn't do your homework. Do you wanna tell the others what happened? You have a funny story, don't you?

2. **Student 1:** Oh God. So ridiculous. No no no no this is so funny. I went to visit my dad in Pennsylvania, which is like a six hour drive away. . . . First of all, I'm the biggest nerd anyway *<laughter>* because I brought all of my stuff, right? So I had my backpack full with like all the stuff that I needed, all of my stat stuff, all the stuff for these tests that I had this week. I get about halfway back here and about three hours into the drive and I'm like oh my god I left my entire backpack.

3. **Student 2:** On top of the car.

4. **Student 1:** No, I left it at my dad's. . . . So I stopped, I got off at an exit. I didn't tell you this part. I got off at an exit, called him from a pay phone and he was laughing at me. He's like I can't believe you left this here. You must be freaking out. I'm like mhm. *<laughter>* So he he airmailed my backpack to me. I got it yesterday afternoon but like, I was already way behind in this and in uh, all my other classes that I have tests in so, whatever.

5. **Student 2:** Jee-

6. **Student 3:** Listen to my story, I'm still behind.

7. **Student 1:** So funny.

8. **Student 3:** Got this stomach infection. I had to go to the emergency room, like this was like three weeks ago. I'm still trying to catch up. I missed an exam and I had a paper due and I got behind in stats. I'm still like behind on my stats like trying to catch up.

9. **Instructor:** Oh life.

10. **Student 3:** But my GSI's[4] like really nice *<laughter>*. Then I still hafta do this make-up test. It's just one thing, it's just one thing after another.

11. **Instructor:** We're never prepared, are we?

12. **Student 2:** College'll do it to you.

(Based on MICASE. Statistics Office Hours, File ID: OFC575MU046)

1. In Excerpt 1, what appears to be the storyteller's attitude toward homework? How about the storytellers in Excerpt 2?

2. What do you think is the underlying purpose of each story?

3. In the second excerpt, the students are attending office hours. Why? Why do you think the instructor begins the session by asking a student to tell her story about her homework?

---

[4] GSI stands for Graduate Student Instructor. Graduate students who teach are also called teaching assistants or TAs.

4. In Excerpt 1, what do these expressions mean?

- So, on Friday I'd *hit the books*.
- *I was a wreck* when I graduated.

In the first story in Excerpt 2, what do these expressions mean?

- I'm the biggest *nerd*. (Turn 2)
- You must be *freaking out*. (Turn 4)

5. In Turn 4 of Excerpt 2, the speaker uses the word *like* a number of times. How is it being used? What does the speaker mean by *so, whatever*?

6. Turn 8 has an example of ellipsis. What word is missing? (See Units 1 and 5 for more discussion of ellipsis.)

7. In Turn 10, why does the group laugh?

8. In Turn 10, what does Student 3 mean by *it's just one thing after another*?

9. In Turn 12, Student 2 says, *College'll do it to you.* What does the student mean by *it*?

10. Some names of course subjects or fields of study are abbreviated in spoken academic English. For example, in Excerpt 2 the students talk about *stats* as a short form for their Statistics class. What about the following classes or units? How could you shorten them?

Economics		Architecture	
Literature		Biology	
Chemistry		Anthropology	
Natural Sciences		Business School	
English Composition		Calculus	

11. Tell a homework story about yourself to your group or class, or ask a friend or instructor if they have a homework story to tell.

Student attitudes toward how much help or advice they can ask for when doing homework or preparing for longer papers also varies. In one study it was found that native speakers of English are more apt to ask their instructors to give them feedback on a first draft of their papers. Non-native speakers tended to submit their final draft and ask for feedback if the instructor is willing to give it (Biesenbach-Lucas 2005). Getting comments on a draft of a paper can be helpful. If you decide to ask your instructor to look at a first draft, be sure to give him or her enough time to read it before the due dates. Consider listing questions that you might want the instructor to specifically address.

Complaining

Complaining is common among students, and its purpose can go beyond the literal intent of the complaint. It can be used to establish rapport or connections with other students.

Task 15

This excerpt is from a philosophy seminar. With a partner or group, read the excerpt, and then answer the questions.

Student 1: I love how like, I love how I'm like the only one who read the assignment, seeing how I usually never, you know I usually do my homework just right before I come to class.

(Based on MICASE. First Year Philosophy Seminar, File ID: SEM475JU084)

1. How is the student using the expression *I love how* in this excerpt? Is she happy, critical, angry, ironic, or sarcastic? What kind of facial expression do you imagine she has?

2. How is *I love how* used in these examples?

   a. *I love how* Pat uh um uh Pat comes late to the meetings but then gets mad when someone else is late.

   b. *I love how* you answered you answered uh that question in class. The instructor was surprised you knew so much about the topic.

   c. *I love how I love how I* I get a good grade one day and then a bad grade the next.

3. The short excerpt contains fillers (words or sounds that don't provide content), some repetitions, and false starts. What are they?

4. How would you compare your study habits to this student's?

Complaints can be either direct or indirect. In a direct complaint (DC) the speaker confronts someone who is thought to be in a position of repairing a problem. For instance, students may make a DC to their TA in response to an exam they felt was overly difficult. Indirect complaints (ICs), on the other hand, can be defined as expressions of displeasure or dissatisfaction about someone else/something for which the listener is not responsible and therefore cannot remedy (Boxer 1993). ICs can also be made about oneself. Here are examples of ICs between two students:

This exam was ridiculously hard.

There was so much reading for today. How were we expected to do it all?

There's no way I'm going to get this project finished. There is just too much to do.

ICs may also be referred to as whining, griping, or moaning. Regardless of the term used to describe them, in most cases (as much as 75 percent of the time) the purpose of ICs is to establish rapport and build solidarity with the listener (Boxer 1993). ICs can also simply give people something to talk about (e.g., complaining to strangers about the weather or a lengthy wait for something). In other words, we complain in order to establish relationships with people (e.g., complaining to others in the class about how difficult an exam was). Given this purpose, you may find that you can increase your opportunities to interact with your classmates by complaining about things or by appropriately responding to their complaints. You may also find your opportunities to interact with your classmates may be decreased if you do not recognize complaints or respond to them in an expected manner.

Task 16

Discuss these questions with a partner.

1. Do you think ICs are common in all cultures?

2. If you are familiar with a culture other than that of the United States, what role do ICs play in that culture?

3. How do people respond to ICs in that other culture?

There are a number of ways you can respond to an IC directed toward you.

1. no response, non-substantive response, or topic switch (not acknowledge the complaint)
2. questions (ask for more information; encourage the complainer to elaborate)
3. contradiction (disagree that there is anything wrong or defend the object of the complaint)
4. joke/teasing (make the situation seem less serious)
5. advice/lecture (help find a solution)
6. agreement/commiseration (indicate a shared concern; express agreement; acknowledge the situation being complained about) (Boxer 1993, 1996).

Task 17

From time to time, students complain about the amount of homework their professors give, as in the following discussion among the members of a math study group. The three students are senior undergraduates. Read the discussion, and then answer the questions that follow.[5]

1. **Jane:** Alright. . . . Why did she give multiple parts for every single problem we have?

2. **Amy:** She wanted to torture us.

3. **Nick:** I think it's cuz like, that last time I don't think we did a lot on the homework, if I remember right.

4. **Jane:** I really like how she says this problem set contains a total of four problems. It's like no, four times two plus one problems.

5. **Nick:** Yeah why does she tell us it contains four problems? She's trying to trick us into thinking like oh. . . .

6. **Jane:** Yeah she's like "Oh that's not bad. This problem set only has four problems in it." Yeah, whatever.

7. **Amy:** And there's like two parts for three of 'em.

8. **Nick:** Alright, so, oh my gosh so this has three parts.

9. **Jane:** For all of 'em?

10. **Amy:** Two parts for all of 'em?

11. **Jane:** Yeah. And number two has three parts.

12. **Nick:** This has three parts.

13. **Amy:** Oh you've got to be kidding.

14. **Nick:** Well at least we only have to do two of the five parts on fourteen. No, this won't necessarily be that hard.

15. **Jane:** Did you say two of the five parts on fourteen?

16. **Nick:** Yeah we only have to do one and two out of five.

17. **Jane:** Oh, alright.

18. **Nick:** And on fifteen we only have to do two of, well one out of four but it's number two. Why don't we. . . . Fourteen's gonna be easy let's start there. It really is gonna be easy.

19. **Jane:** Oh yeah alright.

(Based on MICASE. Math Study Group, File ID: SGR385SU057)

---

[5] This exercise has been modified from one developed by Sheryl Leicher and John M. Swales.

1. In Turn 1, Jane begins by asking a question. Does she expect an informative answer?

2. What kind of responses do Nick and Amy make after Jane's initial complaint about the homework? Do they respond in one of the six ways suggested on page 42?

3. Jane gets two responses. Which one might she prefer, and why?

4. How similar (or different) are Nick's and Jane's attitudes toward the homework? How did you decide?

5. How would you characterize Jane's *I really like how* opening statement in Turn 4?

6. In Turn 6, Jane says something that is transcribed with quotation marks around it. This expression is what is sometimes called *a pseudo-quotative*. What do the quotation marks indicate?

7. At the end of Turn 6, Jane comments, *Yeah, whatever.* What does she mean by *whatever*?

8. In Turn 13, Amy says, *Oh, you've got to be kidding.* What other expressions would have gotten her point across?

9. Would you say that this type of complaining episode is common among undergraduates?

Of the six different response types, agreement/commiseration is the most likely to encourage discussion. This makes sense because commiserating with someone shows that you are concerned, understand the nature of the complaint, and know how the other person is feeling. The type of response least likely to lead to further interaction is a failure to acknowledge the complaint. If a complaint is met with no response or perhaps only a yes or oh with no indication of interest, it's very hard to sustain an interaction. Take a look at these two examples and notice how the second one is more successful at keeping the interaction going.

EXAMPLE 1

SI: I really can't stand doing this project.

S2: Mmhm

SI: I mean I just don't have time for all of this.

S2: *<nods>*

EXAMPLE 2

SI: I really can't stand doing this project.

S2: Mmhm. Me too. These things always seem to be assigned when you have no time to do them.

S1: Yeah, I just don't have time for all of this. I've got a paper due tomorrow and an exam the day after that.

S2: *<nods>* Whoa. How are you going to manage? I mean. That's a a lot.

S1: I'll manage somehow. How about you? What's your schedule like?

Can you think of responses for S2 in Example 1 that might be better than those given in Example 2? Consider the possibilities on page 42.

In the first example, S1 wants to interact with S2, but S2's participation in the interaction is so minimal that S1 stops talking. S1 may even think that S2 is unfriendly, when in fact S2 may simply have not known how to respond. In the second example, S2 commiserates with S1, thus extending the interaction.

The next task focuses on a rather long excerpt of a discussion among students in a French Cinema seminar. As you read through the excerpt, notice how the complaints allow the discussion to evolve.

Task 18

Underline all of the complaints. How do the other students respond to them? Are they using any of the six kinds of responses described on page 42? Which ones?

1. **S5:** You know what you're doing for the summer?
2. **S2:** I'm gonna go to Africa.
3. **S5:** Oh.
4. **S4:** So you're going back?
5. **S5:** Well.
6. **S2:** Yep. [**S4:** Excellent] I got, I got money again so I'm going again.
7. **S5:** Great.
8. **S2:** Yay.
9. **S1:** That'll be awesome. Back to um,
10. **S2:** And um mhm back to Niger.
11. **S4:** Oh yay.
12. **S2:** Same place, same, house probably.
13. **S4:** Who do you stay with when you go or, where do you stay when you go there?
14. **S2:** I stay um, with the woman who's the program director of my study abroad. But, I um, hope that I'll find someplace else.
15. **S4:** Cool. What do you do there?
16. **S2:** I take classes in the mornings, from eight to twelve, and then,
17. **S5:** What classes?
18. **S2:** Hausa. Hausa language class.
19. **S5:** Oh.
20. **S2:** Um, which is, fun but kind of painful cuz it's four hours just me and a professor and
21. **S1:** Oh it's just the two of you?

22. **S2:** Yeah. No books. They don't have any text books. <**S4:** *laugh*>

23. **S5:** Is it, is it your like your research area?

24. **S2:** One of 'em yeah. And so, and then in the afternoons, I just have fun. Enjoying like a good museum, or just wander, go stay someplace air-conditioned, [**S5:** Ah nice.] I love it. So,

25. **S5:** How 'bout you?

26. **S4:** I don't know yet. I'm I think I'll probably go back to Chicago my parents live there and I think I'm gonna try and teach French at like a community college type thing, [**S2:** Oh that's good.] I don't know. What else I see I have this I really like working with autistic kids and that's what I do every summer, [**S5:** Mhm] and I might do that again this summer. I'm not gonna do the same program but, I wanna work one-on-one with autistic kids. Cuz it's fun, [**S5:** That's great] and I don't really wanna do French. <*laugh*>

27. **S2:** Yeah.

28. **S5:** I have no idea.

29. **S2:** No idea?

30. **S4:** No?

31. **S5:** Well my, the memo to the department for, you know that kind of funding is due tomorrow and I'm gonna forget [**S2:** Ohh] about that deadline until Monday. [**S2:** Right] [**S4:** Ah yes.] Um, I gotta, I gotta figure out something because, I um, last year I got money, and I was uh two months in Paris and one, one month in Vienna. It's a . . . humiliating to have to write for more money, [**S2:** Yeah] to say that well, you know generous as it was last year <*laugh*>

32. **S5:** So I gotta figure out, what I'm gonna, see I don't think I can get two months out of them. [**S2:** Right.] [**S4:** Yeah] You know maybe, three weeks max. [**S4:** Mhm] um, but um. I just hate having to look for money.

33. **S2:** I know. I hate applying for summer money. [**S4:** I know] It's always such a, big deal.

34. **S5:** Yeah, deadlines and everything. All those forms. I know this sounds really pompous but I just don't wanna work, this summer. [**S4:** Yeah] I just want a break. I'm tired of studying and I want time off.

35. **S2:** Yeah, that's why I go to Africa because I take, you know, language classes and just have fun and hang out. [**S5:** Yeah yeah] I don't actually do anything regarding, with books. <*laugh*>

36. **S4:** It's all good. Yeah, this summer I need to read read read read I need to get one of those like boring jobs like, nine to five, probably in a book store where they'll give me a nice big discount. [**S2:** Mhm] And then just read all day that's all I'm gonna have to do. [**S2:** Yeah] Find a job where I can just read all day. <*students laugh*>

37. **S2:** That's no fun.

38. **S4:** No it's really not. It's terrible. But, I've had a great summer job the last five years so, I guess I'm, [**S2:** Yeah] I'll get a really bad one this summer. I just need to make money, that's the thing. Paying stupid rent in this town.

39. **S2:** Oh yeah, I know what you mean.

40. **S5:** Mhm.

41. **S2:** Too expensive.

42. **S4:** Yeah it is.

43. **S5:** The beer is expensive too. It's so, it's most annoying.

44. **S4:** I guess that's one benefit of being allergic to alcohol.

45. **S2:** You're allergic to alcohol?

46. **S4:** I am. Most unfortunately. [**S5:** Oh no] I mean I can have like a little you know like, if I'm eating, like wine with dinner, alright, no problem, like a glass. But, I can't drink any beer whatsoever I think the hops in that makes me crazy. Like right off the bat cuz I can't even tolerate like one or half of a beer and then

47. **S5:** Well what happens when you drink it?

48. **S4:** I get really ill. [**S5:** Oh] Like violently ill. And it's not even fun you know it's [**S5:** Yeah] like, you know. [**S2:** It's not even fun *<laugh>*] It's not even fun first and then you get sick. *<laugh>*

49. **S5:** That's so unfortunate.

50. **S4:** I know. But I have gotten used to it over the years.

(Based on MICASE. Graduate French Cinema Seminar, FILE ID: SEM545MG083)

In the discussion, the students are doing a lot to keep the conversation moving. Did you notice the many questions and the feedback indicating that they were engaged in the discussion? How were the transitions from one main speaker to another made?

DVD Task
Unit 2: Homework
Scenes 1–3

In the first scene, a group of students is talking about the challenges and expectations related to homework at college. In the second scene, a group of students is complaining about the homework for a particular class. In the third scene, a group of students is complaining about their courses and instructors.

Imagine you are with friends who begin to complain about their assignments, courses, or instructors. Would you participate? Why or why not? What might you say about an assignment, course, or instructor you have had? Share one of your own experiences with your group.

Expectations Regarding Grades and Grading

Students may also have different attitudes toward their grades. Some students may not have a lot of interest in taking a particular course and therefore may not be concerned about getting a high grade. Other students may strive to get good grades in all their courses. No matter what a student's attitude toward grades is, it is helpful to know the criteria an instructor will use to grade students.

Task 19

In this excerpt from an Introduction to Astronomy discussion section of undergraduates, the Graduate Student Instructor (GSI) (or TA) discusses the criteria she takes into account when assigning grades. With your partner answer the questions.

> **GSI:** Your discussion grade will be thirty percent of your total grade for the course, so generally, you'll want to not waste your time here. Thirty percent is a pretty big chunk, but generally it'll pull people's grades up. Homeworks are generally easier than exams so this is a good place to bring up your grade for the course. Plagiarism is one way that you can bring down your grade for this course. Plagiarism is when you write something and it's not your own ideas or your own words. So we'll do a lot of group work in here. . . . You'll talk with each other, you'll ask questions and that's good. That's why we're here. The problem though is when you write down word for word the same answer to a homework as somebody else, or you have the same diagram, and I can't tell if you copied it or if you actually came up with it yourself. So to discourage, people copying from one another, um I'll give a zero to anybody who copies a homework. So if you have questions about what it means to write in your own words, talk with me about it now, or this coming week, or sometime before it becomes an issue.
>
> (Based on MICASE. Intro Astronomy Discussion Section, File ID: DIS150JU130)

1. How will the GSI (TA) assign grades for the discussion section of the course?

2. The GSI (TA) tells students they should write their own words or make their own diagrams. Does this match her definition of plagiarism?

3. What's your attitude toward your grades? Do you foresee any problems you might have if you were in this discussion section?

4. How are grades determined in your courses?

Students who are not doing well in classes often discuss their grades with their instructors, TAs, GSIs, or advisors. The instructor or advisor can often offer advice that will help the student improve in the future. An advisor can also offer advice related to the bigger picture of a student's life at school, in terms of what classes to take or not take, and how grades might affect future choices or decisions.

Task 20

This interaction takes place at a walk-in session in a dormitory. The student, who is in his junior year, is looking for advice from the advisor. He isn't doing well in his calculus class. Read the interaction, and answer the questions.

1. **Advisor:** So you have a D-plus in Math 105 right now.

2. **Student:** Yeah. . . . And. . . . I have to make this decision. . . .

3. **Advisor:** And there's a question of mastery involved here too. I mean [**Student:** Right] how confident are you feeling about pre-calc concepts at this point?

4. **Student:** This new chapter, like I'm I'm understanding. And the stuff from before, I mean I got a C-minus on the last test, but that's. . . . partly because there are a couple things I was fuzzy on, [**Advisor:** Mhm] and then, um, like I didn't do enough of my homework.

5. **Advisor:** You mean you didn't turn it in or you didn't finish it?

6. **Student:** Well he doesn't he doesn't collect it.

7. **Advisor:** Oh yeah. You were supposed to keep on it yourself. Okay.

8. **Student:** Yeah, yeah. So, so like I mean right now I've started you know working with a friend where we do our homework together which, you know [**Advisor:** Which helps]. That way I know if I'm doing it right or not. . . .

9. **Advisor:** Before the test.

10. **Student:** Yeah before the test *<advisor laughs>* exactly. But I mean the question is. . . . if I get like a B-minus or a C-plus on the test, there is a chance that I'd get a C-minus in the class but [**Advisor:** Mhm] I mean I don't want a D-plus in the class.

11. **Advisor:** I don't think anybody would want that.

12. **Student:** So I mean is a C-minus equally as bad?

13. **Advisor:** No, C-minus is a little better than a D-plus [**Student:** A little better. *<laughs>*] I think . . . I'm hearing a couple things. One is that it took you a while to sort of figure out how to study for this class, [**Student:** Yeah *<laughs>*] how to keep on top of it. And now you kind of have a handle on that, and you understand things that you can do to keep yourself on track. [**Student:** Right] Um, and if you have a question or a problem it's so much better to talk to the GSI ahead of time and, say I'm not understanding this than to do it after the test because you can use the information you get ahead of time [**Student:** Right] to do well on the test. Um, but now now you were thinking are you still thinking of transferring to the Business School though?

14. **Student:** Yeah.

15. **Advisor:** Okay. I mean cuz I I think you've got you got a couple of different implications, neither one of them are particularly easy. Okay if you decide that you want to withdraw from this course because you were doing poorly, you would then need to repeat the course. You're you're probably gonna end up having to defer your admissions to the B-school. They're not gonna make a decision on you until all of your prerequisites are done for the most part, [**Student:** I see] unless you just, if you get a C in everything they'll just reject you outright. Um, . . . it's not as though getting one C or a C-minus is gonna totally kill you [**Student:** Right] if you're also doing well in your other classes and you do well in other things.

16. **Student:** Well right but as far as "well" in other classes like wh- what is the quasi-definition of that?

17. **Advisor:** Well for the business school G- G-P-As are usually between like a [**Student:** Like a three] a three-three three-four you know, so a B-plus A-minus.[6]

18. **Student:** Right. *<laughs>* Well to me that's good.

19. **Advisor:** So what for you is doing well if?

20. **Student:** Doing well is like a B B-minus. . . .

21. **Advisor:** Okay well, the B-school is a little more rigorous . . .

(Based on MICASE. Academic Advising, File ID: ADV700JU047)

1. What does GPA mean?

2. Are you familiar with a grading system in another academic culture? Describe the system.

3. What decision does the student need to make? Why?

4. While the student is speaking, what feedback cues does the advisor give? In other words, how does the advisor indicate that she is listening? When the advisor is speaking, how does the student indicate he is listening?

5. In Turn 3, how does the advisor approach the problem?

6. How does the advisor approach the issue of homework and the student's apparent failure to do the homework in the past? Is she critical of him or does she respond more supportively? Does she directly offer any advice?

7. The advisor mentions that the student is interested in going to the business school. Why is this an important topic?

8. What is the advisor doing in turn 15? Do you think this is important?

9. In Turn 15, the advisor begins to consider the implications of the student's decision. How does she express the various conditionals?

---

[6] In this grading system, A is equal to 4, B to 3, C to 2, and D to 1.

10. In Turn 16, the student asks *what is the quasi-definition of that?* What is he referring to?

11. How is *well* being used in Turns 15–21?

12. Does the advisor give the student any indication that he will eventually be admitted to the B-school?

Many readers of this transcript have commented that the advisor is taking a "kid glove" approach with the student. In other words, the advisor is being very tactful, careful, and cautious in dealing with the student. In fact, this is precisely the approach that advisors will generally take in office hours, particularly when the student is having some difficulty. Given that this is the likely approach of your academic advisor, you should feel comfortable going to him or her. Much more on office hours can be found in Unit 4.

Student Services

Many students feel comfortable going to their instructors or advisor for help regarding their class work. In addition to their instructors, students have many other kinds of assistance available to them. Services for students include health care, assistance for disabled students, and clinics for students needing academic help. Also available are a variety of events, such as musical concerts and plays, and organizations and clubs. When students are new to campus life, they may not be aware of what services are available to them.

Task 21

Work with a partner or partners to collect information about one service on campus. Follow these guidelines in preparing for an interview. Prepare a short presentation to share with other members of the class so that they have a broader idea of the types of support services available to them.

1. CHOOSE A TOPIC

Before choosing a topic with your group, you may wish to do some preliminary research. Which of these services are offered on your campus? Which ones are you personally interested in knowing more about?

- International center
- Career planning office
- Student legal service
- Disabled student services
- Language laboratory
- Psychological counseling center

- Musical or theater society
- Student mediation services
- Recreation center
- Public safety and police services
- Peer-to-peer mentoring program
- Study academic skills center

2. PLAN THE INTERVIEW

As a preliminary step, your group should be able to find information on various campus services by going to the Internet or by requesting a brochure or other written information. However, in order to gather more information about the service you chose, set up an interview with a contact person who works in that service area or knows about the service area. Prepare the interview, remembering to review the interview guidelines from pages 26–30. Think about these reminders as well.

- Plan how long the interview will be and where it will take place.
- Prepare follow-up questions, but be ready to "go with the flow" of the interview. Don't feel tied to your original questions.
- If you are interviewing someone as a group, plan ahead who will take notes and who will start, so you will appear organized.
- Consider writing a thank you note to the person you interviewed, and send it either by email or regular mail.
- Plan how to contact the interviewee if you find you need clarification of any information later.

3. PRESENT THE INFORMATION

Use the form on page 53 to help you organize your in-class presentation.

Pronunciation Focus: Question Intonation

Introduction

Questions usually follow a common pattern of intonation (the rise and fall of your voice). Yes-no questions generally have rising intonation, while *Wh*-questions (those that include a *Wh*-word, such as *who, what, when,* and *where*) are marked by falling intonation as in a statement.

If your intonation pattern is different from what a listener expects, you could be conveying something that you do not intend to convey. For example, falling intonation on a yes-no question could indicate that you are annoyed. Rising intonation on a *Wh*-question could indicate surprise or a lack of comprehension of something just said. Rising intonation on statements that are not intended to be questions could be perceived as a lack of certainty on your part.

Group Presentation:
Finding Out about Student Services

Service, organization, or event: _____

Group Members	Presentation Responsibilities

Main message: _____

Do you think you should use a visual or handout to help show your audience? If yes, what kind of visual would be most effective? _____

Wh-Questions

In a *wh*-question, the intonation falls on the last relevant word that is stressed at the end of the question.

When did you arrive in the U.S.?

What was the most difficult adjustment for you?

How are you doing now?

Yes-No Questions

In a yes-no question, your voice should rise at the end.

Are you glad that you came here to study?

Is the university pretty much like what you expected?

Are you doing okay in your classes?

Either-Or Questions

Either-or questions have rising intonation before *or* and falling intonation after *or*.

Has your adjustment been easy or difficult?

Are you taking mostly math or science courses?

Would you like to go first, second, or last?

Data Collection and Analysis

Part 1: Transcription

With one or two partners, listen to Unit 2, Student Life, Scene 1 or 2 on the DVD, and then choose one to two minutes of speech with questions to transcribe. Each of you should transcribe what you hear, listening to the DVD as many times as you need. You can listen together or individually. Once everyone is done transcribing, compare your transcriptions and try to create a complete transcript of the section you chose. Listen to the DVD again if necessary. Indicate any places in the recording where you cannot figure out what is being said and ask your instructor for some assistance.

Part 2: Analysis

With your partners, mark the questions and the intonation (rising or falling or rising/falling). Write your observations on question intonation.

Part 3: Report to the class

Your report should provide the following information:

1. Remind your listeners of the focus of your investigation.
2. What, if anything, made it difficult to identify the questions and/or intonation of the questions? Was it the recording? The speakers' rates of speaking? Characteristics of the speakers' pronunciations?
3. What are your group's observations on question intonation? What, if any, other interesting pronunciation observations did your group make?

Part 4: Production

With a partner, read aloud and/or role-play your transcript, paying special attention to question intonation.

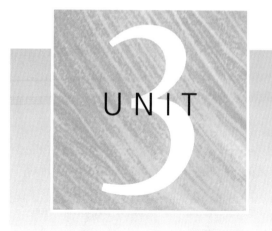

UNIT 3

Communicating by Email

According to recent estimates, more than 50 percent of the U.S. population uses email every day to communicate with others. On college and university campuses, this percentage may in fact be much higher as students communicate with their instructors, other students, and staff members in addition to friends and family.

Email is an interesting form of communication because the language of email has characteristics of both written and spoken language (see page 58). In addition, our reasons for using email mirror the reasons we engage in face-to-face or phone interactions. For instance, we may need to ask questions (e.g., the time and location of a meeting), make requests (e.g., help with homework), or remind others of something that needs to be done. Many of the considerations that result in successful phone or face-to-face interactions also apply to email. Therefore, in this unit, much of the advice given for writing successful email messages will also apply to successful spoken interactions.

While email may appear to be quick, convenient, and easy to use, it can actually be quite challenging to write effective and appropriate email correspondence in an academic environment. The main goals of this unit are to provide some guidance for writing successful academic email messages and to focus on some communicative events that are common to both email and face-to-face or phone interactions. For the latter goal, we specifically focus on requests, apologies, and reminders. By the end of the unit, you should be able to

- write clear subject headings
- use conventional greetings and closings
- make appropriate requests
- give reminders
- offer polite apologies and explanations
- effectively organize and eliminate unnecessary information from your email message.

Email Correspondence: Some General Thoughts

Before we look in detail at some strategies for writing good email messages, there are a few general points we'd like to make. First, it's important to keep in mind that any email message you send could be copied or forwarded to others. Because confidentiality cannot be guaranteed, it is wise to be cautious about discussing matters of a confidential or personal nature in email. Private matters may be better communicated in person or perhaps on the telephone.

In addition, if you participate on listservs and other discussion forums, remember that it is easy to accidentally send messages to the entire group rather than to an individual. A message accidentally sent to an entire group can sometimes lead to embarrassment or could even cause harm that cannot be easily undone. For instance, a listserv member replied to a message sent by a friend, thinking she was replying only to the friend, not the entire group. The personal message included information about an upcoming conference, but in addition to these comments she also asked questions about the friend's recent divorce and health problems. Needless to say, both the sender and the intended recipient were embarrassed. To avoid potential embarrassment, it's best to keep private and professional messages separate and to be cautious when using the reply options.

Also keep in mind that email can easily be misinterpreted. Because email is often composed and sent quickly and is missing the cues available in face-to-face communication, misunderstandings can occur that can lead to hurt feelings or anger. If you are upset by a message, do not reply to it right away. Wait until you are less irritated, then compose a response, read it carefully, and make changes to prevent a breakdown in communication. In some cases, not replying or talking directly with the sender of the message may be a good option.

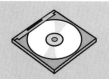

DVD Task
Unit 3: Communicating by Email
Scenes 1–2

In these scenes, students are talking about using email to contact their instructors. In the first scene, a student is unsure about how to contact her professor; in the second scene, a student wants to get an extension of her project deadline.

In Scene 1, what specific advice does Jake give Angie about emailing her instructor?

The Spoken and Written Nature of Email

Email correspondence has features of both spoken and more formal written English, which sometimes poses a challenge when it comes to vocabulary and grammar choices. This lack of a clear distinction between spoken and written English also has the potential to lead to miscommunication. By being aware of the less formal (i.e., spoken) and more formal written characteristics of email correspondence, you will reduce the chances of your messages being misunderstood and feel more confident about your ability to compose appropriate email messages for academic purposes.

Task 1

With a partner or small group, list some features of spoken English, or conversations, and features of more formal written correspondence in English. Write your ideas in the chart. If the same can also be said of email, place a check (✓) in the email column. Then discuss the questions and share your ideas with the class.

Features of Spoken English	Also in Email?	Features of Formal Written English	Also in Email?
not always planned	✓	edited and polished	✓ (?)

1. In what context might a face-to-face encounter be easier for you? For instance, if you need to make an appointment with your instructor, would you ask him or her in person?

2. When might email be easier?

3. Which do you prefer overall when you need to communicate with someone? Does your preference depend on the person you need to interact with?

As discussed in Task 1, email combines features of both written and spoken language. It can be said that some email exchanges are like having a written conversation. A considerable amount of research has been done on conversational language, some of which might apply to email. For instance, the philosopher Paul Grice proposed four conversational maxims, or principles, that arose from the pragmatics of natural language (1975). They operate on the idea that successful communication in conversation happens when the speakers follow certain cooperative principles. Speakers might ignore or violate the principles for a specific intentional reason (to convey humor or irony, for example), but if they violate the principles unintentionally, communication can break down.

Grice's Maxims are summarized here.

Maxim of Quality: Truth
- Do not say what you believe to be false.
- Do not say that for which you lack adequate evidence.

Maxim of Quantity: Information
- Make your contribution as informative as is required for the current purposes of the exchange.
- Do not make your contribution more informative than is required.

Maxim of Relation: Relevance
- Be relevant.

Maxim of Manner: Clarity
- Avoid obscurity of expression.
- Avoid ambiguity.
- Be brief.
- Be orderly.

Task 2

Which, if any, of Grice's principles do you think clearly apply to email? Why? Discuss with a partner.

We will refer to these principles throughout this unit, showing how their application can help communication. However, it is also important to remember the role culture plays in communication. What might be considered relevant or appropriate in one culture may be the opposite in another culture. We need to be aware of how what we write may be perceived by the reader, taking into account such factors as our relationship to the reader (including the reader's status) and the purpose and tone of the message. Some messages we send to instructors may strike them as overly personal, demanding, or detailed. In addition, we may not have considered the email expectations an instructor has established. What we will cover in the rest of the unit will focus on what is socially, culturally, and linguistically appropriate for academic email in the context of a U.S. college or university.

Task 3

With your partner or group, discuss these questions.

1. What are some reasons that you email your instructor? What do you worry about most when writing email in an academic setting?

2. Have you noticed any cultural differences in email communication?

3. What do you think is a reasonable amount of time to expect a reply from a spouse or family member? A close friend? Your department secretary? Your instructors? What would you do if you sent an email message to your instructor but didn't get a response?

Email Subject Headings

The subject heading in an email message to your instructor can serve the important purpose of indicating the content and relative importance of your message. It is not uncommon for email users to receive 50 or more email messages each day, many of which are "junk" or "spam." Messages with blank or vague subject headings are less likely to be opened. A well-written subject heading indicating the general purpose of your message helps to make sure that your message is seen and answered. However, writing a heading that summarizes your message is not always easy.

Task 4

Here are some subject headings sent by students to their instructors on class-related topics. With your partner or group, discuss which headings for Situations 1 to 3 you think are acceptable or unacceptable and why. Keep in mind Grice's Maxims. Then write your own subject headings for Situations 4 to 6 and show them to your partner or group for comments.

1. *Situation: The student is having trouble with a homework assignment.*

Please help me	Help
I need help with Chemistry homework	Question abt hmwk
Any time to help?	

2. *Situation: The student has to miss class.*

Sorry about absence	I'll be absent Weds.
Take one day off	Ask for leave
I'm sick	

3. *Situation: The student is sending his homework to the instructor in an attachment.*

Academic Writing Class	Paper
Homework 2	Revise
Homework for Academic Writing	

4. *Situation: You want to email your instructor to ask for help finding a topic for your psychology paper. What subject heading would you write?*

   Subject: _____

5. *Situation: You want to email your instructor to explain your absence from the previous class.*

   Subject: _____

6. *Situation: You want to email the first draft of your paper to your instructor in an attachment.*

   Subject: _____

When replying to a message, the original heading is carried over under *Subject* or *RE* (the standard abbreviation for *in reference to* or *regarding*). Keeping the same subject heading in a series of email messages lets the reader know that you are continuing to correspond on the same topic. However, if you change the focus of the message, it is preferable to use a new subject heading so as to avoid confusion.

Emailing Your Instructor

There are a variety of ways to open and close your message, depending on your relationship to the sender and the purpose of the email. Some may be formal, for example, if you are emailing the head of your department about scholarship applications; others may be very informal, for example, if you need to email your good friend about the assignment in a class you are taking together. This next task focuses on appropriate openings and closings for email correspondence.

Task 5

Answer these questions with this situation in mind: you are writing a message to your instructor to explain why you can't attend class.

1. One study found that 41 percent of native speakers of English did not put a greeting in their email to their instructor while 76 percent of non-native speakers did use one (Biesenbach-Lucas 2005). What is your opinion about beginning an email message to your instructor with a greeting?

2. What are some greetings that you could use?

3. Would you identify yourself? If so, how?

4. What are some ways you could close your message?

5. If the correspondence involves several messages back and forth to your instructor on the same topic, would you advise including a greeting each time? If you do include a greeting in a series of messages, would you use the same one throughout or a different one?

6. What do you think of the following greetings, identifying sentences, and closings? Place a check (✓) next to the ones that seem appropriate. With your partner or group, discuss which options you chose and why.

Greeting

_____ *Dear McDonald,*

_____ *Hi Professor,*

_____ *Dr. Jim,*

_____ *Dear Madam,*

_____ No greeting

Identification

___ *I am Wei Chen.*

___ *This is Wei Chen. I am in your Chemistry 258 class.*

___ No identification

Closing

___ *Thanks a lot, Wei Chen*

___ *All the best, Wei Chen*

___ *Love, Wei*

___ *Regards. Wei Chemistry 258*

___ No closing

After the closing, you might choose to add an electronic signature. An electronic signature is a feature of an email program that, if activated, will be included at the end of every message you send. It may include a full name, title, address, phone number, or other contact information, as in the following example.

> Charles Lee, PhD
> Associate Professor, Dept. of Mechanical Engineering
> Room 1013 Engineering Bldg.
> University of Michigan
> Ann Arbor, MI 48109
> (734) 555-4567 phone
> (734) 555-7654 fax

In some cases, a signature can be very useful if it provides relevant contact information. It is also possible to personalize the signature with a quote, a saying, or even a short poem. We suggest using caution when choosing these personal additions to the signature. When considering whether to personalize a signature or not, ask yourself how this quote might be viewed by the reader. For example, if you had a quote that reflected a specific political belief and the recipient of the email held very different beliefs, what impression might that create? You may want to consider removing the personalized quotes after a signature when you are sending email for professional purposes.

Task 6

Here are some quotes that have appeared in electronic signatures. With your partner, discuss whether or not these would be appropriate to use in an academic context. Why or why not? What impressions might you have of the person who chose these quotes?

1. "Reduce, Reuse, Recycle"

2. "Chance favors the prepared mind." Louis Pasteur

3. "All we are saying is give peace a chance." John Lennon

4. "Injustice anywhere is a threat to justice everywhere." Martin Luther King, Jr.

What would you think about quotes from religious books? Movies or television? Fiction or poetry? Politicians?

Email Requests

One reason students write their instructors is to request help. In fact, many instructors encourage their students to write them with requests related to their academic work.

Task 7

Look at these two email requests. What purpose does each sentence serve? What do you think are the most effective features of these email messages? For ease of reference, sentence numbers have been added.

Message 1

(1) Subject: Request for recommendation

(2) Dear Professor Garcia,

(3) I'm applying for a study abroad program in Spain this winter. (4) They asked me for a letter of recommendation from one of my Spanish professors. (5) The deadline for the letter is in 3 weeks. (6) If you're not too busy, would you be willing to write me a letter of recommendation? (7) If you can help, I'll send you the format for the letter.

(8) Thanks a lot.

(9) Muchas gracias,

(10) Brian

Message 2

(1) Subject: Help on paper topic

(2) Dear Sandra,

(3) I've been trying to decide on a topic for the final paper in your course. (4) I have three ideas for topics and would like to get your input. (5) I was wondering if we could meet outside of office hours because I have a class at that time. (6) I'm free Monday, Wednesday, and Friday afternoon.

(7) Thanks for your help,

(8) CJ

In addition to the greeting, thanks, and identification, typical features in a polite request are

- the context or reason for the request
- the specific request (often in the form of a question)
- an acknowledgement that the recipient may not be able to honor your request (often in the form of a conditional if clause), or that you are imposing on the recipient
- any necessary additional details, including options for the recipient.

Politeness in Requests

Whether you make a spoken request by voicemail or in person or via an email message, you are more likely to get a positive response to your request if you are polite. Although the concept of politeness is quite complex, here we will offer some suggestions for achieving an appropriate level of politeness in both spoken and email requests.

Task 8

Consider this situation: An instructor wants to talk to a student after class because the student has not turned in several assignments. The instructor can choose a number of ways to formulate that request as well as choose whether to send an email message or talk to the student directly. Place a check (✓) next to the requests your instructor might email you and those that might be said to you in person. With a partner, discuss each of these in terms of how polite the request is.

Email	Face-to-Face	
		See me after class tomorrow.
		Please see me after class tomorrow.
		Would you please see me after class tomorrow?
		Would you be able to meet me after class tomorrow?
		I've noticed that you haven't turned in much homework lately. I'm available after class to talk.

Would your choices change if the roles were reversed? In other words, which of these requests would be appropriate if you wanted to see a professor after class?

Although you may have learned that *please* is polite, it can in fact be a bit tricky to use. In some cases, *please* is perceived as polite, but in other situations, it could have just the opposite effect on your email recipient. In an email message, *please* may seem inappropriate because you cannot use the intonation often associated with politeness. Take this example:

> *Would you please give me your feedback by tomorrow?*

This request has some of the elements of a polite request: the use of the modal *would,* the question form, and *please*. However, it may be seen as demanding for two reasons. One is that the request itself may be asking more than is reasonable. Another is that it is possible to read the request with stress on *please,* which could suggest irritation or annoyance on the part of the sender.

In spoken English, the placement of *please* within the request as well as a particular kind of intonation and facial expression may also be a signal of displeasure. It has been argued that when *please* is placed at the end of a sentence it may be perceived as more polite than when it comes after the subject in a question, but here again intonation is still important.

> Could you give me more time to finish the homework, please?
>
> Could you please give me more time to finish the homework?

If you use an imperative to make a request, it may likely be considered impolite (Brown and Levinson 1987) whether it includes a *please* or not. Take a look at this:

> Please send me a copy of the handout.

This request, while grammatically correct, could be offensive because it looks more like a command. The person sending it would appear to be pushy (overly demanding).

Fortunately, there are a few things you can do to avoid a possible negative reaction to your email or spoken request.

- Use modals (e.g., *could;* however, the modal alone may not be enough to make sure your message does not appear overly demanding).
- Acknowledging that your request may be burdensome to the reader (e.g., *I know you are busy, but . . .*).
- Begin the request with an expression that is less direct, such as *I was wondering whether you. . . .* (Note the use of the past tense here.)
- If you are making a request in person, you may want to begin with a "pre-request" before making the actual request:

> Can I ask you a favor? Would you be able to . . . .
>
> Can I ask you something? I'm having trouble with . . . . Could you help me figure out . . . ?

- Use an expression related to possibility.

> Would it be possible for you to . . . ?
>
> Is there any chance that you . . . ?

- Make it possible for the other person to say no (e.g., *If you don't have time that's OK).*
- Re-consider whether your request is reasonable or not. (Do you recall how busy the professor was in Unit 2?)

Look at these requests that students have made to instructors, asking for some feedback on a paper. The requests in the column on the left would likely be considered appropriate because they are deferential and courteous. The requests in the right column may be seen as inappropriate because they come across as demanding. They seem more like demands than requests.

Appropriate	Demanding
Can you send me the feedback via an attachment?	I want you to send me the feedback via an attachment.
Could you send me the feedback via an attachment?	I'd like you to send me the feedback via an attachment.
Would it be possible to send me the feedback via an attachment?	Please send me the feedback via an attachment.
I was wondering if you'd send me the feedback via an attachment.	Send me the feedback via an attachment.

Task 9

How about these requests? Which column would you put them in? Why? What might it depend on? Mark them A for appropriate or D for demanding.

_____ Just send me the feedback via an attachment.

_____ Would you send me the feedback via an attachment?

_____ Could you please send me the feedback via an attachment?

_____ Would you mind sending me the feedback via an attachment?

_____ How about sending me the feedback via an attachment?

_____ You had better send me the feedback via an attachment.

_____ I was wondering if you could send me the feedback via an attachment.

Just as Grice's Maxims are important in spoken and written communication, so are another set of principles knows as Leech's Maxims of Politeness (1983). When you make a request (email or face-to-face) or engage in any other kind of interaction, the maxims should generally apply.

Leech's maxims are summarized here:

Tact Maxim: Minimize the imposition or the cost to the other.

Generosity Maxim: Minimize the benefit to yourself (don't emphasize how much you will *personally* benefit).

Approbation Maxim: Minimize dispraise (i.e., criticism) of others.

Modesty Maxim: Minimize praise of self.

Agreement Maxim: Minimize disagreement between self and others.

Sympathy Maxim: Minimize antipathy (i.e., bad will) between self and others. Pay attention to the hearer's interests, wants, and needs.

Consider these maxims as you complete Task 10.

Task 10

This section contains a set of five email requests from non-native speakers of English to their instructors and advisors. Read them, and with your partner or group, answer the questions that follow.

Message 1

Subject: Make an appointment

My Dear Advisor,

This is Ken. I have some questions about courses next semester. I think it will be very helpful to discuss with you. Could you kindly squeeze some time to help me? Thank you very much.

Regards,
Ken

Message 2

Subject: Have an Appointment

Dear Henderson,

This is Catherine from your 330 class. I have something to request you. Would you mind if you give me feedback about the first draft of my term paper? It's attached I was wondering if I could make an appointment with you. I'm free tomorrow afternoon. PLEASE CAN YOU EMAIL ME TODAY?

Catherine

Message 3

Subject: My CV

Dear Terry,

Thanks for offering to correct my curriculum vitae. Here I attached my file. Please send me back no later than Thursday. The earlier the better though. I have to mail it with the application on Friday.

Sincerely,

Ken

Message 4

Subject: Reschedule test

Dear Sir:

My name is Francisco Gonzales, new student in mechanical engineering this year. I need to take the oral Academic English Exam on August 31 but I have the department orientation that day. So I write to you and want you schedule a time for me tomorrow, anytime is OK. I have no schedule. If tomorrow is not available, please schedule some other time.

Thank you very much

Francisco

Message 5

Subject:

Hi, Kim,

How was your semester break? I had to write a paper over break and it is due Friday. Could you help me revise it? I think you are the best reviser. If you don't have time, I'll try to find someone else. The file is attached. I can meet with you any time after 11:00 Wednesday or Thursday.

[no closing]

1. Do any of the requests appear to be unreasonable?

2. Do you think the greetings and closings are appropriate? If not, how would you change them?

3. In which messages do you think the writer appears to have made an overly direct or demanding request? What changes would you make? Does the wording of any of the requests seem awkward?

4. Which messages take into account the instructor's situation?

5. What message do you think is the most successful? Least successful? Why? Does your choice have to do with the student's grammatical, spelling, or vocabulary errors? How important are these types of errors?

If you have a request that has a deadline, such as a due date for a paper or letter of recommendation, it is especially important to make this clear—for example, *The letter needs to be postmarked by March 15* or *My paper is due on February 1*. Leave enough time for a request to be carried out before the deadline.

Email has changed our expectations regarding the amount of time to wait before getting a response. In fact, we may expect and even demand immediate replies or action. When writing an instructor or advisor, it is important to consider that he or she, because of other responsibilities and obligations, may not respond in what you think is a timely manner.

Some Advice on Making Appointments

Native speakers of English are more likely to give their instructors options for times they can meet than non-native speakers are (Biesenbach-Lucas 2005). When requesting an appointment, it is helpful for the instructor to know specific dates and times you are available, giving several options to help the instructor better schedule the meeting. When you make a request via email, you don't know when your email will be read; therefore, time expressions such as *today* or *tomorrow* should be avoided. Instead, using specific days/dates such as *Thursday 11/15* or *tomorrow, Friday the 10th* is more helpful.

Task 11

Discuss with a partner which of these requests for an appointment would be considered polite. Specifically, consider whether all of the statements before and after the actual request are necessary or helpful. Mark the messages that you think are fine with a + and those that could be improved with a –. If you and your partner disagree place a question mark (?) in the blank. As you discuss each item, consider the different maxims introduced earlier.

_____ 1. Hello, Professor. How are you? It's such a lovely day. I have been enjoying the wonderful sunshine. How about you? I would like to talk to you about the paper I'm writing for your class.

_____ 2. I hope that we can make the appointment tomorrow. I just don't know what to do to prepare. Without your excellent advice I will surely fail the exam. I would appreciate it very much if you could understand my situation.

_____ 3. I have a question about the homework. I've done everything but Part 4, and this is what I'd like to discuss. So, can we meet some time this week?

_____ 4. I am in the middle of writing my paper and I need to talk to you. You are my advisor and the only one that can help me. My paper will be so much better with your input. I will stop by your office tomorrow at 1:00.

_____ 5. I know you have many other important things that you are busy with, but could you spare me some of your precious time? I think if you have 5 minutes that will be enough.

_____ 6. I think you didn't grade my exam properly and took too many points off of Question 4. My friend only lost 1 point, but I lost 3 for the same response. I need you to explain why. Can I see you after class tomorrow?

_____ 7. I was wondering whether I could meet you after class tomorrow. I have a question about my score on the last quiz.

_____ 8. I'm confused about the concepts you covered in class today. Would it be possible to see you some time Thursday or Friday afternoon?

Task 12

Compose three email messages, each of which includes a request. You may choose from the situations given or choose situations of your own. Be sure to include the subject heading and an appropriate opening and closing. Bring a copy of your messages to class or actually send the practice email messages to your instructor, depending on what your instructor wants you to do. If you do send the messages we suggest preceding your subject heading with something like HOMEWORK to indicate it is an assignment.

1. You want to take a class, but the class is full and you are not able to register. Ask the instructor if he or she will give you permission to take the course. Explain your situation.

2. You would like to return to your country for winter vacation on December 20 because it is the last date you can get an inexpensive airline ticket. Unfortunately, you have an exam on December 21. Explain your problem to the instructor and suggest a solution.

3. You didn't do well on the last exam and you want to meet with the instructor.

Speaking Option

Working in groups of three or four, choose two students to role-play a face-to-face interaction based on one of the situations given in the email task (or another situation of the group's choosing). While the two students are doing the role play, the other one or two students should observe them and give feedback. The observers can comment on such aspects as the level of detail, choice of grammar or vocabulary, body language (especially eye contact), and anything else worth pointing out. Observers should point out aspects of the role play that were done well and those that could be improved. After your group discusses the feedback, role-play and observe again or ask the observers to role-play.

Messages in Response to Awkward Situations

What would you do if you sent a message to your instructor or advisor requesting a favor but never got a reply? Would you assume that the receiver decided not to write back, forgot to write back, or never got your message? It could be very uncomfortable to be in the situation where you need to remind someone that they forgot to do something or missed a meeting with you. However, there are certain politeness strategies you can learn to use so that you feel more comfortable handling these awkward situations.

Task 13

Read these examples of reminder messages from students to their instructors, and then answer the questions. Refer to both Grice's and Leech's politeness maxims.

Message 1

Dr. Armstrong,

I went to your office for our appointment today at 2:00 but you weren't there. I hope I didn't get the time wrong. Can we reschedule? I can meet in the afternoons after 2:00.

Thanks a lot,

Anton Federov

Message 2

Hi Mr. Hendricks,

Thanks for your message. I think you forgot to attach the article.

Jaehoon

Message 3

Dear Dr. Lum,

I hope you had a good weekend. I wrote you last week to ask you if you could meet with me about my paper, but I haven't heard back from you. Maybe you didn't get my email. I'm still free on all day Thursday and Friday. Can you see me this week so I can work on the paper over the weekend?

Sincerely,

Alex Chen

Message 4

Dear Robin,

The Chemistry Department hasn't gotten the letter of recommendation you were going to write for me. It's due in two days. I know you are busy but could you send it as soon as possible. I really appreciate your doing this.

Thanks,

Sofia Gouvas

1. What politeness strategies do these students use in their reminder messages to their instructors?

2. In Messages 3 and 4, what strategies do the students use to encourage their instructors to respond to their request?

3. What subject heading could you use with each of these reminders?

4. How might you deal with these situations in a face-to-face interaction? With your partner, choose one and write a short dialogue and be prepared to present it to your class or a small group.

Task 14

Compose three email reminder messages. You may choose from the situations given or choose situations of your own. Be sure to include the subject heading and an appropriate opening and closing. Bring a copy of your messages to class or actually send the practice email messages to your instructor, depending on what your instructor wants you to do. If you do send the messages, we suggest preceding your subject heading with something like HOMEWORK to indicate it is an assignment.

1. Your instructor wants the class to read several articles for class next week but forgot to post them on the class website.

2. You are a little disappointed with your advisor. You wrote her a week ago, and she has not gotten back to you. You want to fulfill your language requirement by taking French. But you would like to find out if you can skip French I. You studied last summer in France and think you are ready for French II.

3. Your instructor said that he would look at the first draft of a paper you are writing for class. You sent it via an attachment and asked him to let you know when he had finished looking at it so that you could meet with him. A week has gone by and you haven't heard from him.

Speaking Option

Working in groups of three to four, choose two students to role-play a face-to-face interaction based on one of the situations given in the email task (or another situation of the group's choosing). While the two students are doing the role play, the other students should observe them and give feedback. The observers can comment on such aspects as the level of detail, choice of grammar or vocabulary, body language (especially eye contact), and anything else worth pointing out. Observers should point out aspects of the role play that were done well and those that could be improved. After your group discusses the feedback, role-play and observe again or ask the observers to role-play.

Apologies in Email and Speaking

As a student, there may be times when you cannot fulfill your obligations—for example, you forget to go to a scheduled appointment or can't get your work in on time. In such cases, you may feel that you should apologize.

The typical features of an email apology include:

- greeting
- the apology
- a brief explanation or excuse
- your action plan (what action you will now take)
- another apology in closing (optional)
- closing.

Do you think these same features are typical of a face-to-face apology? What about an apology you leave on someone's voicemail?

Useful Language for Apologies

We begin by looking at *to be sorry* used in apologies. It is of particular interest because the grammar used with it is quite varied.

1. *to be sorry + for*
   a. *I'm sorry for the delay.*
   b. *I'm really sorry for being late.*

   Which of these forms can be used with a present or past situation? What about a future situation?

2. *to be sorry + about*
   a. *I'm sorry about missing class.*
   b. *I'm sorry about having interrupted so much yesterday.*

   Which of these forms can be used with a present or past situation? What about a future situation?

3. *to be sorry + to*
   a. *I'm sorry to ask for more time to finish my paper.*
   b. *I'm sorry to be taking up so much time.*

   Which of these forms can be used with a present or past situation? What about a future situation?

4. *to be sorry* + *that* clause

    a. *I'm really sorry (that) I was late.*

    b. *I'm sorry (that) I'll miss class next Friday.*

<u>Note</u>: In spoken English, *that* is commonly omitted.

Which of these forms can be used with a present or past situation? What about a future situation?

In spoken English, *I'm / I am* is often omitted. (See Unit 5 for more detailed discussion about ellipsis.) So, you will often hear something like, *Sorry for being late.*

It is also possible to use the verb *to apologize* as in the following examples. Note with the verb *to apologize, that* is generally not omitted.

1. *to apologize* + *for*

    a. *I apologize for the delay.*

    b. *I apologize for having missed class.*

2. *to apologize* + *that* clause

    a. *I apologize that I was late.*

    b. *I apologize that I don't have my book.*

Task 15

Choose three of the apology forms discussed, and write three one-sentence apologies for both of these situations.

<u>Example situation</u>. You lost the book your roommate let you borrow.

a. I'm sorry for losing your book.

b. Sorry about losing your book.

c. I'm sorry to have lost your book.

d. Sorry (that) I lost your book.

e. I apologize for losing your book.

Situation 1. You turned in the homework late.

a. _____

b. _____

c. _____

Situation 2. You did the wrong homework assignment.

a. _____

b. _____

c. _____

Check the MICASE database to see how common *sorry* and *apologize* are. For each word print a section of a transcript where the words are used. Bring your findings to class.

_____

Now that you are familiar with some of the language used for apologies, let's look at how it is used in context.

Task 16

This section contains a set of five email apologies from students to their instructors. Read them, and then, with your partner or group, answer the questions that follow.

Message 1

Subject: late for assignment

Dear Kart,

I'm sorry for not being able to hand in my assignment on time. To tell the truth, I had three midterms this week. I pulled an all nighter but still couldn't get your homework done. I can do it this weekend and give it to you in the next class.

Sorry for bothering you.

Sue

Message 2

Subject: Missing assignment

Dear Professor Williams!

I would like to apologize for not handing in the homework for today. I really finished it but I couldn't retrieve it from my server because the system wasn't working. I tried calling the computer help line but it was constantly busy, probably because everyone else was calling to find out what was wrong. Just when it was working again, it was time for class. So I decided not to be late for class and just come without the homework. I am really sorry about not having the assignment. If you don't mind, I'll send it to you tonight or tomorrow morning.

Sincerely,

Doug

Message 3

Subject: absence today

Professor,

I would like to apologize for being absence at your class today. I had to pick up parents up at the airport because they've never been to the U.S before. I know I was supposed to make my 3-minute presentation. I am really sorry about that. Can I do it next class?

[no closing]

Message 4

Subject: Sorry for missing class

Dear Instructor.

I regret to inform you that I won't be in class tomorrow because of a religious holiday. One of the students in the class is taking notes for me and will let me know the assignment.

Sincerely yours,

Elie

Message 5

Subject: I have to miss class

Hi,

It's too bad I couldn't show up to class today. ☹ I stayed at home to get my high-speed internet hooked up. ☺ Did I miss anything important?

Thanks, Gisela

---

1. Do you think the greetings and closings are appropriate? If not, how would you change them?

2. Underline the language used to make the apology. Could any of them be improved?

3. Do the apologies seem sincere and the explanations/excuses acceptable?

4. What action plans seem adequate?

5. In what messages do you think the writer could have shortened the excuse?

6. Does it appear that the email messages have been checked for vocabulary and spelling errors as well as other typos? Does it seem the names of the recipients are spelled correctly?

The expression *I regret to inform you* is generally used to convey bad news. It is not considered an apology but rather expresses regret about an unfortunate situation. The expressions *it's too bad* and *it's a pity* should not be considered an apology because the speaker does not appear to take responsibility for the circumstances. You may also be aware that *sorry* can also be used to express sympathy, as in *Sorry about your bad grade* or *Sorry to hear you were sick.* These are not apologies.

It may not be necessary to make an apology in some situations, such as missing class when your instructor doesn't seem to have a policy regarding absences and does not take attendance (like in large lecture classes). Also remember not to promise something that is impossible, such as *I will never miss your class again,* or *I will never be late again.* While your intent is good, it is not something you can promise will never happen.

It is particularly useful to keep Grice's Maxims of Quantity and Relation (Relevance) in mind when writing apologies. For instance, extended excuses with excessive details are not necessary and, in fact, can even be somewhat annoying. Unnecessary repetition or details should be avoided. Here are some examples, with the repetition and excessive detail crossed out.

I'm sorry I can't come to class today because I have a cold ~~and need to stay in bed. I think I have a fever too. That's why I have to miss class~~.

Please forgive me for missing our appointment. ~~It snowed this morning and the roads were slippery and I was very nervous about driving~~. Because the roads were icy and I don't have much experience driving, it took me a long time to get to campus, so I missed the appointment.

Task 17

In these messages, cross out information you think is repetitive or provides more detail than is necessary. Think about how much information the instructor really needs. Explain your decisions to a partner. Also discuss whether the excuse is acceptable or not.

Message 1

Subject: missed Tuesday's class

Dear Professor Jacobson,

I would like to apologize for missing class on Tuesday. I know I should have told you in advance but I was just so busy preparing for my oral exams that I couldn't think about anything else. These exams are really important for me and I was worried about how difficult they might be. So I spent the whole past week studying for them and missed my regular classes, including yours. So now the exams are over. I think I did pretty well, actually. And I will start to concentrate again on this class. I will come to your office hour tomorrow to see what I missed.

Again my apologies,

Richard

Message 2

Subject: I was sick

Dear Sarah,

Sorry I had to miss class last week. As you know a lot of students are sick these days because of the flu and I got it too. I went to the Health Services and the doctor ordered me to rest in bed and not be around too many other people, or I might get them sick. The flu is really contagious he said. So I'm taking medicine and now I feel better but still I am pretty weak. I think I will be strong enough to come to class this week, so don't worry. I will ask my classmate about what I missed. Is it OK if I come to your office hour too? Thank you for your understanding.

Sincerely yours,

Sri

Message 3

Subject: Conflict with class

Hi,

I thought I could make it to class in time but I had another commitment that took longer than I thought it would. The guys from Best Buy were delivering my new home theater system and said they'd come in the morning. I thought that meant like before 10 but they came at noon almost. So I missed class because I had to wait for them to get to my house and install it. I couldn't just let them leave it on the porch! Well, you know how it goes so I hope that's ok.

Thanks,

Peter R.

Speaking Option

Take one of these three messages, and transform it into a dialogue in which you apologize face-to-face to an instructor.

Task 18

Compose three email messages, each of which includes an apology and an explanation. You may choose from the situations given or choose situations of your own. Be sure to include the subject heading and an appropriate opening and closing. Bring a copy of your messages to class or actually send the practice email messages to your instructor, depending on what your instructor wants you to do. If you do send the messages, we suggest preceding your subject heading with something like HOMEWORK to indicate it is an assignment.

1. You missed a meeting with your advisor to go over courses for the upcoming semester.

2. You couldn't finish the assigned paper in time to turn it in on the due date.

3. You are always late to English class because the class you have before it is quite far away across campus.

Speaking Option

Working in groups of three or four, choose two students to role-play a face-to-face interaction based on one of the situations given in the email task (or another situation of the group's choosing). While the two students are doing the role play, the other students should observe them and give feedback. The observers can comment on such aspects as the level of detail, choice of grammar or vocabulary, body language (especially eye contact), and anything else worth pointing out. Observers should point out aspects of the role play that were done well and those that could be improved. After your group discusses the feedback, role-play and observe again or ask the observers to role-play.

Emoticons and Abbreviations

Sometimes students use emoticons in emails to their friends and family. Emoticons are symbols mainly used to express feelings. The word is a combination of the words *emote/emotion* and *icon*. The verb *emote* means to express feelings in a theatrical or exaggerated manner. Some common emoticons include:

Happy/Smiling:	☺ :) or :-)
Sad:	☹ :(or : -(
Angry:	X(
Confused:	:-/
Laughing:	:-D

In addition to conveying feelings, emoticons can also be used to send abbreviated messages. For example, <:-P is a symbol for party.

Abbreviations are also commonly seen in email, particularly personal or informal correspondence. Some common abbreviations include:

FYI:	for your information
ASAP:	as soon as possible
BTW:	by the way
LOL:	laughing out loud OR lots of love
U:	you
TTYL:	talk to you later

Task 19

With a partner or partners, discuss whether you should use emoticons or abbreviations in your email messages to: your instructors, your friends, a potential supervisor, and an instructor whom you do not know.

Even though emoticons may convey useful information to the reader about the intended meaning of the message, they are generally not included in academic email. There may be cases in which a smiley face or another emoticon can be used appropriately, but caution is recommended.

The first three abbreviation examples are relatively common and could be found in academic contexts. The latter three examples are quite informal and likely would not be seen as appropriate in an academic email to your instructor, for example. With the popularity of instant messaging on computer or text messaging on cell phones, these kinds of abbreviations are becoming widespread, and often find their way into email correspondence. As with emoticons, caution is recommended in using abbreviations in academic contexts.

Online Course Discussions

In some of your classes, you may be asked to participate in online course discussions. In these cases, you may be asked to give your opinion on a particular topic. The strategies taught in Unit 6 on how to offer your opinion and acknowledge other points of view can be used in online discussions as well.

Research shows that students who are reluctant to speak in class find online discussions offer them an opportunity to participate in ways they might not otherwise. In online discussions, there is no pressure from the instructor or your peers to come up with something on the spot. Because you have time to compose your thoughts in a non-threatening or safe environment, you may feel better able to participate in the discussion. Participating in online discussions is a good first step that can lead to more confidence in the classroom setting.

Pronunciation Focus: Acronyms

Introduction

English is full of acronyms—words that are formed from the first letters of a series of words or groups of letters from a series of words. Common acronyms that you may already know are AIDS, DVD, CEO, and OPEC.

It's not always clear how to pronounce an acronym. For instance, why are CEO and LED pronounced by saying each individual letter even though it is possible to say these like any ordinary word? We're not aware of any rule that applies, but usually if an acronym can be pronounced like an ordinary word, then we tend to do so. Exceptions likely arise if there is a potential for a lack of clarity. Thus, to be absolutely sure about pronunciation of acronyms in your field or your college or university, it may be best to ask someone who is knowledgeable.

Listed here are some different kinds of acronyms, some of which you may already know.

ACRONYMS PRONOUNCED AS WORDS

ANOVA

CAD

GIF

ACRONYMS PRONOUNCED USING INDIVIDUAL LETTERS (BUT NO BREAKS BETWEEN THEM)

The stress is fairly equal across all of the letters but is usually slightly stronger on the final letter, which is considered the focus.

ACT

FAQ

ASAP

FYI

PDF

BA

HYBRID ACRONYMS

Hybrid acronyms are pronounced in part like a word and in part using initial letters (with no breaks between the word and the letters).

Usually, the stress is fairly equal across all of the letters but is slightly stronger on the first letter. (CD-ROM is different, however. The stress is somewhat stronger on ROM.)

CD-ROM

JPEG

GMAT

LSAT

IELTS

MCAT

ACRONYMS WITH REPEATED LETTERS

Usually the stress is on the final letter.

AAA (triple A)

IEEE (I-triple E)

AAAL (triple A-L)

CCCC (four C's)

Data Collection and Analysis

Part 1: Data Collection

With one or two partners, come up with a list of 10 acronyms that are important in your academic environment. For each of the 10 acronyms, write sentences placing the acronym in mid-position. For instance, you might write the following:

I listen to some lectures on my MP3 player.

My group is working on improving HEV technology.

Be sure to RSVP by next week.

I got my MA six months ago.

Ask two or three native speakers to look over your sentences and get some feedback from them in terms of the usefulness of the acronyms and the sentences you generated. Ask the native speakers to read the sentences as informally as they can and ask for their permission to record them. Record the speakers. Play back your recording to check that it is okay.

Part 2: Transcription

Write what you hear when the native speakers say the acronyms. Indicate any places in the recording where you cannot figure out how the acronym is being pronounced.

Part 3: Analysis

With your partners, discuss the pronunciation of the acronyms. Write your group's observations on pronouncing acronyms in context.

Part 4: Report to the class

Your report should provide the following information:

1. Remind your listeners of the focus of your investigation.
2. How did you collect the data?
3. What, if anything, made it difficult to hear the acronyms. Was it the other words surrounding the acronyms? The recording? The speakers' rates of speaking? Characteristics of the speakers' pronunciations?
4. What are your group's observations on pronouncing acronyms in context? What other interesting pronunciation observations did your group make?

Part 5: Production

With a partner, read aloud your sentences, paying special attention to how you pronounce the acronyms.

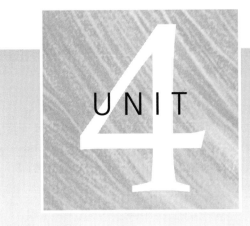

UNIT 4

Interacting with Instructors and Advisors: Office Hours and Appointments

This unit focuses on interacting one-on-one with instructors and advisors. We'll begin by looking at why students go (or do not go) to office hours. We will then move on to what goes on in office hours and how to leave an office hour. Because students often go to office hours to get advice, one important part of this unit is recommendations, advice, and suggestions. By the end of this unit you should be able to

- understand the purpose of office hours
- negotiate a meeting time
- prepare for an office hour
- indicate your academic interests
- offer and understand typical responses to *thank you*
- apply strategies for leave-taking
- understand types of advice or recommendations.

Students often wonder what they can do to be successful in their undergraduate or graduate degree programs. Of course, it makes sense that students should attend class regularly, take good class notes, do all assigned homework, and study using available resources (lecture notes, readings, practice tests, and so on). However, many students do not realize that one of

87

the keys to success is interacting with their instructors outside of class. In fact, nearly every guide to college success highlights the importance of talking with instructors and going to office hours. Faculty members are expected to have office hours, during which time they are available to help students. Because office hours provide a one-on-one, confidential opportunity for students to talk with instructors, this time can be an extremely important aspect of learning. During office hours, students can talk about the course material, get some help with homework or test preparation, and build a relationship with an expert.

According to a study in the *Journal of Applied Communication Research* (Bippus et al. 2003), 68 percent of students engaged in at least one interaction with their instructor outside of class. Most of these encounters were initiated by students, were face-to-face (41.8 percent) or conducted by email (28.5 percent), and were primarily course related.

Task 1

Discuss these questions with a partner or partners.

1. Do you think the percentages given indicate a lot of or little student-instructor interaction outside of class?

2. Why do you suppose 28 percent of the students used email to interact with their instructors?

3. Why do you think nearly 30 percent of students had no interactions with their instructors?

4. Have you ever gone to an instructor's office hours? Why or why not? If you have gone, describe your experience. Do you think your visit was successful? Why or why not?

Certainly to a large extent, the behavior of your instructors in class can encourage or discourage you from having contact with them outside of class. If your instructor seems approachable, then you are more likely to seek some interaction with him or her. You may be less likely to try to meet your instructor outside of class if he or she is not on campus very often, does not return email or phone calls, or does not seem particularly interested in talking to students before or after class.

Task 2

Here are some perceptions that might affect your decision to go to office hours. Discuss with a partner whether you agree (A) or disagree (DA) with the statement in relation to your instructors.

_____ 1. My instructor doesn't seem to have time outside of class for students' concerns.

_____ 2. My instructor is on campus a lot.

_____ 3. My instructor is available before and/or after class to meet with students.

_____ 4. My instructor discourages student contact outside of class.

_____ 5. My instructor tells the class to come to office hours or make appointments to talk.

_____ 6. My instructor seems interested in knowing the students in the class.

_____ 7. My instructor responds promptly to email and phone messages.

_____ 8. My instructor seems uninterested in responding to student email messages about the class.

_____ 9. My instructor seems to be bothered when students try to talk to him/her outside of class or office hours.

_____ 10. My instructor seems enthusiastic about the class content.

(Based on Bippus et al. 2003)

Regardless of how approachable your instructors may seem, it is still a good idea to visit them during office hours. There are many reasons to consider going to office hours, as highlighted in Task 3.

Task 3

With a partner, discuss which of the situations would prompt you to go to your instructor's office hours. Place a check (✓) in the corresponding blanks.

_____ 1. You are not sure about a couple of ideas presented in the lecture and need some help understanding them.

_____ 2. There is something in the text you read and still don't completely understand or on which you would like to comment.

_____ 3. You want to make sure the instructor knows who you are—that is, connect your face to your name.

_____ 4. You're not sure what to do in order to do well on an exam.

_____ 5. You are in the middle of writing a paper and are not sure you are on the right track.

_____ 6. You know you will miss class and want to find out if the instructor will cover anything important.

_____ 7. You are getting ready to register for the next term and want to know something about courses and professors.

_____ 8. You have a visual impairment or other disability that affects your ability to manage the course requirements.

_____ 9. You finished writing a paper for your class and want your instructor to look over your work before you turn it in.

_____ 10. You are unable to go to the review session for an upcoming exam and want to get some idea of what will be on the exam.

Can you think of some other reasons why you might visit your instructor's office hours? List them here.

_____

For many students, many of these situations would be a good reason to visit office hours. Although you may feel unsure about whether you should go to office hours, if you are aware of the wide range of acceptable reasons to go, you may feel more confident to give it a try.

DVD Task

Unit 4: Office Hour Concerns
Scenes 1–2

In these scenes, students are talking about office hours. In Scene 1, the students are discussing what to do about a difference in how their tests were graded; in Scene 2, a student is unsure about going to office hours and wonders what to do.

Role-play with one or two other students a situation where you might want to go to office hours (e.g., you aren't sure about paper topics/lab partners/project requirements). Use some of the language you heard in Scene 1 of Office Hours.

Task 4

Here are some reasons that students go to office hours. Interview three students who are not in your class to find out whether they think these are good reasons to go to an instructor's office hours. Mark their responses as yes (Y), no (N), or unsure (U). Be prepared to report your findings to the class.

I go to office hours because I want my instructor to . . .			
	Student 1	Student 2	Student 3	
1.				give me good advice about my career.
2.				help me understand what is expected in class.
3.				give me extra information that I don't get in class.
4.				help me get a good grade.
5.				suggest choices in school that will further my career.
6.				help me with my assignments.
7.				let me know about possible job opportunities.
8.				answer questions I'm afraid to ask in class.

(Based on Bippus et al. 2003)

You now have a few ideas of when you should go to an office hour, but what if you have a conflict and need to arrange a special time to meet? Some students would simply not go. Others might try to catch the instructor before or after class. Still others will try to schedule an appointment. What would you do?

Task 5

Read this interaction in which a student is trying to set up a special time to meet with an instructor. Discuss the questions.

1. **Student:** Hi, um I'm Erik. Are you going to have office hours next week before Wednesday?

2. **Instructor:** Um, not before Wednesday.

3. **Student:** Can I meet you earlier? It's about the exam schedule.

4. **Instructor:** Okay. When?

5. **Student:** Monday maybe?

6. **Instructor:** Um, yeah . . . um. . . .

7. **Student:** Whoa. I've got an exam that day. 3:30.

8. **Instructor:** Yeah, and I'm in the lab most of the day. How is noon?

9. **Student:** Noon? Perfect.

10. **Instructor:** In 1156.

11. **Student:** Your office?

12. **Instructor:** Yeah.

13. **Student:** Okay.

(Based on MICASE. Philosophy Discussion Section, File ID: DIS475MU012)

1. It helps to be prepared for an interaction such as this one by having options of times you can meet. Notice how in Turn 4 the instructor wants the student to suggest a time. Which of the following would be good alternatives to the student's response of *Monday maybe?* in Turn 5?

What about Monday?	Monday is good for me.
Would Monday work?	Monday.
I have to see you Monday.	What's best for you?

   Can you think of another response?

2. Why does the student say *maybe* in Turn 5?

3. What does *whoa* mean in Turn 7? Why does the student say this?

4. In Turn 9, notice how the student responds to a question with a question and then indicates that the time will work. What are some other options besides *perfect* for Turn 9?

5. How willing does the instructor seem to set up an appointment with the student?

6. How many of the turns consist of fully grammatical sentences? What elements are missing from Turns 10 and 11? Is any meaning lost because of ellipsis (see Units 1 and 5)?

7. Student 1 in the next interaction needs or wants to see one of his instructors. Read the example to understand why a visit to office hours is necessary, and then work with a partner to create a dialogue to arrange a time to meet between Student 1 and the instructor of the class whose office hours don't fit the student's schedule. (Note the use of *homeworks*. Many students in the United States say *homeworks*, although not so long ago *homework* was considered to be a noncountable noun—not plural.) What does *schedule conflict* mean?

1. **Student 1:** These homeworks, the homeworks. They're just ridiculous, homeworks. They're so hard. [**Student 2:** Uh huh] It would be cool if I could go to office hours, you know. Our homeworks are always so hard, and then I want to go to office hours and then I'm like, hmm okay, but . . . .

2. **Student 2:** Schedule conflict?

3. **Student 1:** Yeah, I can't make it to office hours—ever.

(Based on MICASE. Chemical Engineering Group Project Meeting, File ID: SGR195SU127)

Now finish this dialogue with the instructor in which the student wants to schedule a special time to meet.

Student 1: Uh, Professor Becker, do you have a minute? I have a question about office hours . . . .

Instructor: Yeah, sure.

_____

_____

_____

_____

When you go to office hours to get some help, be sure of what you want to discuss so that you can effectively use your time as well as that of the instructor. For instance, if you are going for help be sure that you have made some prior effort to understand or do the work. If you are having trouble with homework, try to identify the nature of the difficulty you are having with it and have specific questions to ask the instructor. One question that you should avoid asking is *Can you tell me how to do the homework / this problem / this essay?*

Task 6

Here are some examples of questions that can lead to a productive use of time in the office hour. Why are these better than a question like *How do I do this problem?*

1. I've been working on this problem for a long time and I get this far and I am stuck, I can't get this equation to work. What am I doing wrong?

2. I'm not sure I'm doing this problem right. Do you have to assume . . . ? The book doesn't really make it clear.

3. On the second problem, I was wondering if this equation is okay for this kind of circuit. I tried using it since that's what we were told to do in lecture, but then I get this result. And that doesn't make any sense.

4. I'm having trouble understanding the question for this week's reaction paper. It seems to me that it all depends on how you define sustainability, doesn't it?

5. I checked my answers with the ones in the book and they don't match. I was talking to somebody else and they didn't get the same answers as what was in the book either. So, what are we doing wrong? Is there something I'm missing with the input and output temperature here?

6. I'm having trouble following the explanation in the book of how the virus spreads. I understand everything up to here. But can you explain these steps?

If you consider the nature of these questions, you will see that each suggests that the student has done some work before going to the office hour. The students are goal oriented. So, to make the most of your time spent with your instructor, make sure that you have carefully read the assignment, have attempted to do some of the work on your own or with classmates, and have formulated specific questions.

Task 7

Read these three office hour interactions between students and instructors. With a partner, discuss the questions.

INTERACTION 1

1. **Student:** Um I have to, to go away this weekend and I won't be in class on Friday. What should I do to get ready for the exam? I have to leave tomorrow morning, so what should I do? I wanna be ready. I'm going to New York by plane and I wanna do a bunch of practice problems. [**Instructor:** Mhm] So what should I . . . what would you recommend? For the problems.

2. **Instructor:** Well, I would look at exam two that's in the back . . . [**Student:** Okay] back of your book. And I'd take a look at the packet I gave out in class yesterday.

3. **Student:** The one with the new model?

4. **Instructor:** Exactly. There are problem sets in the packet. Um. . . . Tomorrow, we are going through section six of chapter eleven, okay? So in terms of getting ready, I'll be finishing that topic on Friday. [**Student:** Okay. . . section six] Mhm. Eleven, chapter eleven, sections 1–6.

5. **Student:** Is that gonna be on the exam?

6. **Instructor:** Yep mhm mhm. . . .

(Based on MICASE. Statistics Office Hours, File ID: OFC575MU046)

INTERACTION 2

1. **Instructor:** Okay, who's next?

2. **Student:** I'm confused about the homework. I can't find the homework problems that I'm supposed to be doing.

3. **Instructor:** Okay, I, I wrote you an email a last week and when it says homework eight it doesn't mean chapter eight.

4. **Student:** Uh I understand. I looked for the problems in my book and it doesn't have them . . . . [**Instructor:** Okay, okay, okay, okay] the same chapters. Maybe I have an old book.

5. **Instructor:** Well then you have to look on our course website. I can't guarantee that all the solutions are there, but look. The problems are there.

6. **Student:** I thought I looked, though, but I couldn't find them.

7. **Instructor:** Okay, well did you click on the Assignment link? You should see them there.

8. **Student:** Oh, I guess I didn't look there. I should have. I was looking on the resources part. Oops. Okay. Thanks.

(Based on MICASE. Statistics Office Hours, File ID: OFC575MU046)

INTERACTION 3

1. **Student:** Hi, uh, do you have a minute? Can I check one answer with you? Do you have time to check? [**Instructor:** Mhm?] Do you have time to check? I don't think I'm doing problem 7 right.

2. **Instructor:** I have to teach at 11:00 and I'm already a little late. I'm sorry.

3. **Student:** Okay, never mind. [**Instructor:** Um] Could I find you sometime later at maybe around uh between 2:30 and 3:00?

4. **Instructor:** I'm here two-thirty to three. Okay? Alright. And in case you can't find me, I'll try to leave the solutions on my desk. Okay, alrighty. I'll leave them here if you wanna come back earlier, but I'll be back between two and three.

5. **Student:** Okay, thank you. Sounds good.

6. **Instructor:** Okay. Yep. No problem.

(Based on MICASE. Statistics Office Hours, File ID: OFC575MU046)

1. Discuss the apparent reason that each student went to the instructor's office hour. Do you think each of the students really needed to talk with the instructor? Would you go to an instructor's office hour if you had the same concerns as the students? Why or why not?

2. Do the students in each of the three interactions seem prepared for the office hour visit? Explain your opinion.

3. Do you think the language of the interactions is formal or informal? Explain.

4. In Interaction 1 during Turn 1, the instructor says *mhm?* What is the function of *mhm* here? Does *mhm* have the same function in Turn 6 of this same interaction?

5. In Interaction 2, Turn 8, what does *oops* mean? Why do you suppose the student said this? Are there any other expressions besides *oops* that the student could have used?

6. In Interaction 3, Turn 1, the student asks the instructor, *Do you have a minute?* What other ways can you ask someone whether he/she has time for you? List them.

7. In Interaction 3, Turn 4, the instructor says both *alright* and *alrighty. Alright* is an alternative spelling of *all right.* Often *alright* is used to describe something that is good, but not exceptionally good or great: *The class was alright. Alright* is also used as an expression of great pleasure: *I got an A on my exam! Alright!* Does *alright* have one of these meanings here? Why do you suppose the instructor says *alrighty* the second time rather than *alright?*

8. In Interaction 3, Turn 6, what does *yep* mean? Have you heard any other alternatives to *yes* and *no?*

9. In Interaction 2, Turn 2, the student says, *I'm confused about the homework.* Place a check (✓) next to those items that you might use to indicate confusion or a lack of understanding.

_____ I don't get how . . .   _____ I don't get it.

_____ I don't understand why . . .   _____ What do you mean?

_____ I don't see where . . .   _____ I have no idea . . .

_____ How come . . . ?   _____ Huh?

_____ I can't figure out how . . .   _____ I'm (still) lost.

_____ This/that doesn't make sense to me.   _____ What?

_____ (Silence)   _____ I don't understand.

10. In Interaction 2, in the middle of Turn 4, the instructor says, *Okay, okay, okay, okay.* What, if anything, does this repetition of *okay* indicate about how the instructor feels about the student's problem?

11. In Interaction 1, the student is very obvious about wanting to get some information about the upcoming test. However, many students may not want to reveal such a hidden agenda. What do you think is better? Should students be clear about wanting information about an exam or should they be more subtle? What are the advantages and disadvantages of each strategy?

It's also important to anticipate how an interaction with your instructor or an advisor might develop. For instance, if you go to your advisor to talk about your class schedule, you need to think about what classes you are interested in, rather than relying on your advisor to make decisions for you.

DVD Task
Unit 4: Appointments with an Advisor
Scenes 1–3

In these scenes, an academic advisor is meeting with three students with different problems. The first has signed up for too many credits, the second has questions about his course schedule, and the third wants to change her major.

Watch Scene 3. Does the student, Jean, seem ready for the appointment? What is the purpose of her visit? Does the advisor seem surprised by Jean's plan? How do you know? What expressions and/or phrases does the advisor use in response to the plan?

Task 8

Read this interaction between a student and advisor discussing course selection, and complete the tasks that follow.

1. **Advisor:** So, who's next? You are . . . ?

2. **Student:** Hasan.

3. **Advisor:** Okay, Hasan, what's up?

4. **Student:** I need to talk about my schedule for next semester. I need some kind of social science class.

5. **Advisor:** Okay. What kinds of things are you interested in? You're interested in . . . ? What kind of course is it that you want?

6. **Student:** _____

Which of these responses do you think would be the best for Turn 6? Consider which one demonstrates that the student has given the schedule some thought. Which of the responses suggests that the student has not really thought about his or her schedule?

a. I don't know. Uh. Um. I just don't know what to take.

b. Well, uh. I'm kind I'm kind of interested in taking an Economics class.

c. Can I uh take an Economics class? Um I don't know uh if there are any prerequisites like Calculus, but I'd like to try it.

d. I want to take Economics, but I'm worried uh whether . . . whether I can do okay.

e. Is Economics hard?

f. Would Economics be good?

g. Maybe something business related.

Discuss with a partner what classes you'd like to take some day. Some expressions that you might find useful follow.

I'm interested in taking . . .   *I'd like to take a course in . . .*

I want to take . . .   *I was hoping I could take a class in . . .*

I think I'd like to learn more about . . .   *I've always wanted to take a class in . . .*

Typical Organization of an Office Hour

Office hours are intended to help you with a variety of questions, the most common of which center around homework, exams, and grades. No matter what you want to talk about, it is helpful to understand the typical organization of the interaction during an office hour. While there is no fixed pattern of events in an office hour, researchers have observed that many office hours include the following moves.

1. Pre-interaction
   This may be a simple knock at the door or a look to see if someone is in the office.

2. Greeting or perhaps a question regarding the instructor's ability to meet, such as,
   Hi
   Who's next? (from the instructor)
   Do you have a minute?

3. Explanation for the visit

4. Discussion, negotiation, and problem-solving (can be repeated for multiple questions or problems)

5. Close
   Expression of thanks
   Mention of future interaction or intentions (for example, *See you later in class)*
   Good-byes

6. Raising of another issue (Sometimes. If another issue is raised on leave-taking, then Step 4 is repeated.)

(Based on Limberg 2007)

Task 9

Read this interaction during office hours, and discuss the questions with a partner.

1. **Student:** Hi uh, is this a good time? Do you have a couple of minutes? Um um I was wondering if I could turn in my paper a day or two late. I'm gonna be applying for grad school and I'm taking the GRE this week.

2. **Instructor:** Grad school, huh? Well, sure. I can see that you might be doing some last minute studying. What field?

3. **Student:** I think uh um sociology. Maybe. I don't know, but I'm really leaning toward sociology.

4. **Instructor:** So, have you started doing your applications?

5. **Student:** Yeah, but I have to see an academic advisor about a letter of recommendation. I wanted to wait till grades are in cuz hopefully that'll make me look better *<laugh>*.

6. **Instructor:** You know who you should see? Do you have an academic advisor who you know?

7. **Student:** No.

8. **Instructor:** You should go see um, uh Karen Taylor. [**Student:** Karen Taylor] She used to . . . . She was my colleague in the American Culture Program. She's really great. [**Student:** okay] Um, and uh, she . . . probably actually knows about a lot of other programs because she's been a student all over. So she knows professors and stuff. So I'd go see her.

9. **Student:** Alright.

10. **Instructor:** Okay?

11. **Student:** Well, thank you very much.

12. **Instructor:** No problem.

13. **Student:** And uh, you'll get my paper on Monday, and hopefully it'll be good.

14. **Instructor:** I'm sure it'll be good.

15. **Student:** Oh, I have another question.

16. **Instructor:** Alright go.

17. **Student:** *<laugh>* Um . . . would you mind if I borrowed your book to make a copy of that chapter you mentioned in class? I think it might help me with the paper.

18. **Instructor:** Um sure.

19. **Student:** I mean . . . if you have it and it's not a problem to borrow it.

20. **Instructor:** Yes.

21. **Student:** Alright. Okay, cool. Thank you.

22. **Instructor:** No problem. How long do you think you'll need it?

23. **Student:** A couple hours maybe. Can I give it back in class?

24. **Instructor:** Okay. Sure. Later.

25. **Student:** See you in class.

(Based on MICASE. Anthropology of American Cities Office Hours, File ID: OFC115SU060)

1. To what extent does this interaction follow the typical organization discussed on page 99? Try to label the office hour in terms of pre-interaction, greeting, explanation for the visit, discussion, close, and raising of new issue.

2. Who seems to be managing the topics of discussion here? The student or the instructor? Would you be comfortable managing the topic of discussion? Why or why not?

3. In Turn 15, does *oh* seem to convey any particular meaning? If so, what?

4. In Turn 16, what does the instructor mean by *alright go*?

5. In Turns 1 and 17, how polite are the student's requests? Can you think of any other ways to make a polite request? List them.

6. Are there any expressions or vocabulary in the interaction that you find interesting or potentially useful? Do you have any questions about these?

Leaving the Office Hour

Instructor: You know, some students are pretty diligent about coming to office hours. They're there all the time, every week, without fail. On the one hand that's great I mean uh I love how uh I love that dedication, but the other day I had this student come see me, my office hour was 12 to 1 and it was already 1:30 and I have to teach at 2:00. So I so I really had to get my class stuff together, you know, and I need about 15 minutes at least to get to my classroom. So uh, I finally say, "We have about five minutes until we have to stop, uh I've got class soon, so let's try to wrap up." You know I wanted her to pick up on this and realize that I hafta go to class, but she didn't, she was so focused on her paper. So then I kinda obviously check my watch and say "Okay, you know, well, I have class now, so let's figure out when we can meet." Then . . . I actually stood up and started getting my stuff together cuz I really did hafta go. So I then I say something like "Okay, you know, walk with me over to my classroom and then if you need more time, you might wanna email me, email if you wanna meet tomorrow, or next office hours, okay?" And she um, finally picked up on that and we left.

(Based on an ELI instructor's story)

As indicated by this story, knowing when to leave is important. Once you have gotten the help you need, however, you may be unsure of how to leave the instructor's office. Should you just say *thanks* and leave? You may also need to be sensitive to the verbal and non-verbal cues the instructor is sending to indicate that it is time for you to leave.

Task 10

With a partner, discuss the questions.

1. What do you think of the instructor's announcement that he/she had only five more minutes to spend with the person in the office? Would you be so direct?

2. Is the instructor's non-verbal cue of standing up to send the message that time was up polite? Why or why not?

3. What are some non-verbal cues that you think indicate that it's time for a person to leave? For example, if your instructor started tapping his or her fingers on the desk, would you consider this to be a signal to leave?

4. What can you do as a student to indicate that you need to leave?

Although it is possible to end an office hour with a simple *Thanks for your help. See you in class,* leaving an office hour can involve a series of short turns between the participants before one of them actually leaves.

Task 11

Read these two leave-taking sequences between a student and an advisor. Then answer the questions.

LEAVE-TAKING 1

1. **Instructor:** Okay. So we're done?
2. **Student:** Yeah.
3. **Instructor:** Great.
4. **Student:** Great.
5. **Instructor:** I'll just move this here. Don't forget your bag.
6. **Student:** Should we anticipate a quiz on Thursday or?
7. **Instructor:** Uh, you can anticipate. I don't know if there is gonna be a quiz on Thursday actually. I'm not sure.
8. **Student:** Okay.
9. **Instructor:** I'm sorry.
10. **Student:** Okay. So, you would give two quizzes in the same week?
11. **Instructor:** It's . . . no no no this is a make-up quiz.
12. **Student:** Oh okay. I was gonna say . . . *<laugh>*
13. **Instructor:** It's a make-up quiz.
14. **Student:** Okay. Thank you.
15. **Instructor:** Okay. Kristen.
16. **Student:** See you Thursday. *<leaves>*

(Based on MICASE. American Culture Advising, File ID: OFC105SU068)

1. In Turn 4, it seems like the interaction is over, but then in Turn 6, the student raises a question about a quiz. And in Turn 10, the student asks a more general question about quizzes. Why does the student continue to ask questions when it seemed the interaction was finished?

2. Who seems to be keeping the interaction going? The student, the instructor, or both?

3. How long are each of the turns here? Do you think this is typical when an interaction is winding down?

4. In Turn 9, why does the instructor say, *I'm sorry*?

5. In Turn 12, what does *I was gonna say* indicate? Can you guess what the student was thinking?

6. What, if anything, is accomplished during the turns after the student indicates that they are done? Did the student gain anything?

LEAVE-TAKING 2

1. **Student:** So . . . I guess I'll try to get into Psych 215.

2. **Advisor:** Okay. So it looks like we're all set now, right?

3. **Student:** Okay. Good I'll I'll ask about getting into the psych class. Okay great. I think that I'm set then [**Advisor:** Okay] for this semester. Thank you.

4. **Advisor:** Yeah, the teacher, she's very good and really conscientious. [**Student:** Good] She might be difficult to get in to see right now, [**Student:** Okay. Yeah] because she's the only one teaching the class, *<student laugh>* um but, you know, she can definitely answer anything. You can probably make an appointment with her for the end of December or you know, [**Student:** Okay] when you're taking your exams.

5. **Student:** Yeah *<laugh>* Okay that's great.

6. **Advisor:** Okay well that's . . . I'm glad that, things are going well and uh . . . .

7. **Student:** Yeah, I was surprised too that, I guess. What is senior standing? How many credits? Do you need, do you know what the cutoff is?

8. **Advisor:** Um 85 credits.

9. **Student:** Oh it's 85? [**Advisor:** Mhm] Okay I thought it was more than that.

10. **Advisor:** And if you, you know what's nice though is that you can take whatever psychology you want, [**Student:** Uhuh] without trying to take everything.

11. **Student:** Right, exactly. Okay thank you very much.

12. **Advisor:** No problem.

13. **Student:** And I'm sure I'll see you later *<student laugh>*.

14. **Advisor:** I hope so.

15. **Student:** Bye.

16. **Advisor:** Good to see people still smiling at the end of the semester.

17. **Student:** Yeah *<student laugh>*. Thanks.

18. **Advisor:** Buh-bye.

(Based on MICASE. Academic Advising, File ID: ADV700JU047)

1. At what point during the interaction does it seem that the student and the advisor have finished what they needed to do?

2. For how many more turns does the interaction continue beyond the point you identified in Question 1?

3. Who is keeping the interaction going? The student, the advisor, or both?

4. Why do you suppose there are so many turns before the student leaves? What is going on in the additional turns?

5. What is your preference? To leave the moment you have finished your business with your instructor or advisor or linger a little bit? Why?

6. Are the leave-taking turns long or short in your opinion? Do you think this length of turn is typical when an interaction is winding down?

7. What does *all set* in Turn 2 mean?

8. Note how many times the word *okay* is used in each of the two excerpts. What do you suppose the function of *okay* is in these interactions?

Sometimes the student needs to initiate the closing moves to leave the office hour. Task 12 focuses on doing this.

Task 12

Read this interaction, in which the instructor and student are discussing the student's paper. The student has to get to a class and doesn't have much time. What should he/she say next?

1. **Instructor:** So, I think this section is not very clear. I um don't quite get your point. What do you want to say?

2. **Student:** I wanted to say uh. I wanna point out that the cost of some useful technology is so high no one can afford it.

3. **Instructor:** Well, that's a good idea, but where's the evidence? Where's the support? I mean it might be true, but why should . . . you need some concrete example. You know to convince the reader.

4. **Student:** Oh well yeah. I guess I should add . . . .

5. **Instructor:** Examples. Examples.

6. **Student:** Okay I got it. I get it.

7. **Instructor:** Okay good.

8. **Student:** _____

Which of these seem appropriate for ending the interaction? Place a check (✓) by those that do.

_____ I have to be somewhere, so I gotta go.   _____ I have to go now.

_____ Well that's all. I'm going to go.   _____ Thank you. Good-bye.

_____ I have to run to class. Thanks for your help.   _____ Okay, thanks. Bye.

_____ Other _____

_____ Other _____

Does it seem like the instructor and the student accomplished something? What?

 **DVD Task**

Unit 4: Office Hour Appointments
Scenes 1–4

In the first two scenes, the office hour time is limited, and the instructor has to leave. In the first scene, the student does not pick up on this; in the second scene, she is much more aware of the instructor's time constraints. In the third scene, an instructor is discussing choices a student has made in his paper; the final scene is a first-year student seeking advice from her theater instructor.

Analyze Scene 3 between the first-year theater student and her instructor. Does it follow the typical structure of the office hour outlined in the text? If not, how does it differ? Use the transcript of the interaction, and mark where the different parts start and end.

Thank You and *You're Welcome*

In several of the transcripts you've read so far, you might have noticed that the speakers do not always respond to expressions of thanks with *you're welcome.* Instead, they may simply say *No problem.* How common is such a response? What response do you expect when you said *thank you* to someone?

Interestingly, our investigation of the MICASE database suggests that the response of *no problem* is indeed quite typical. In MICASE, there are 310 instances of *thanks* and 455 instances of *thank you.* However, there are fewer than 40 *you're welcomes* in response to expressions of thanks. Of this small number, 21 are in service encounters. So it seems that members of the academic community do not say *you're welcome* very often. It's not wrong to say *you're welcome;* it's just not that common in non-service encounters. One exception is when a speaker says, *Thank you very much.* In this case, you are more likely to hear a *you're welcome* in return.

Task 13

Discuss with a partner.

1. Which of the following have you heard in response to an expression of thanks? Place a check (✓) next to the expressions you have heard.

_____ (no response)	_____ Okay	_____ Yeah/yup/yep	_____ Sure
_____ No problem	_____ Good	_____ All right	_____ Sure thing
_____ Mhmm	_____ You bet		

2. Read each of the interactions, and underline all of the expressions of thanks as well as the responses to them.

END OF AN OFFICE HOUR

1. **Student:** Great. Thanks for your time.

2. **Professor:** Good. Well, I'll see you tomorrow morning then.

3. **Student:** Alright, thank you.

4. **Professor:** It was very nice meeting with you.

5. **Student:** You too.

6. **Professor:** Okay.

7. **Student:** Bye.

8. **Professor:** Bye bye now.

(Based on MICASE. Honors Advising, File ID: ADV700JU023)

END OF A MICASE RECORDING SESSION

1. **Student:** Thanks for the pizza. It's wonderful.

2. **Research Assistant:** Oh, sure. Good . . . thank you for being recorded.

3. **Student:** No problem. We'll do anything for free food, right?

(Based on MICASE. Biochemistry Study Group, File ID: SGR175SU123)

A SERVICE ENCOUNTER

1. **Student:** Hi.

2. **Student at Service Desk:** Hi.

3. **Student:** Here's the key. Can I get my license back? It's like, all I have right now. *<laugh>* Thank you very much.

4. **Student at Service Desk:** You're welcome. No problem. Have a good day.

5. **Student:** Thank you.

6. **Student at Service Desk:** Sure.

(Based on MICASE. Media Union Service Encounters, File ID: SVC999MX104)

3. William Safire, in his "On Language" column for *The New York Times Magazine,* has argued that *you're welcome* "is rapidly disappearing from the language of civility." Another perspective on *you're welcome* is that in many instances where people are thanked, no one has actually done a favor and so *you're welcome* would not be appropriate. For example, if someone is simply performing his or her job duties, then a *you're welcome* may seem unnecessary. Do you agree with either of these two points of view? Why do you think speakers don't use *you're welcome* and instead choose other expressions to respond?

4. When you say *thank you,* you have the option of specifying what you are thanking the person for. *Thank you* can be followed by a noun or noun phrase. For example,

Thanks for the books.   Thank you for your help.

Thanks for giving me the books.   Thanks for helping me.

Note the use of the *-ing* form of the verb to form a noun clause, which takes the place of a noun after *thanks for.* How would you say *thank you* for the following?

a. Your advisor has given you some ideas about good courses to take.

_____

b. Your instructor looked over a paper for you and made some helpful comments on it.

_____

c. Your instructor has let you borrow a couple of books.

_____

d. Your instructor said that he/she would be able to write a letter of recommendation for you.

_____

e. Your instructor has said it would be okay if you turned in an assignment late.

_____

Some Final Advice on Interacting with Your Instructors

- Try to go to the office hours of at least one instructor each semester so that over time you increase your confidence to meet with instructors outside of class.
- Try to take some small seminar classes. Small classes are designed to encourage students and instructors to interact.
- If you live in a residence hall, find out whether the dining halls allow students to invite instructional staff to meals. Many dining halls offer such programs free of charge in order to encourage students and faculty to get to know each other.
- If you are very nervous about meeting an instructor, you can initiate the request via email; you can also ask one or two classmates to go with you to the office hour.
- Some classes may have many sections and several instructors. If you are not comfortable with your own instructor, investigate the possibility of getting help from an instructor of another section.
- Visit a teaching assistant's office hours instead of the professor's hours, if you are reluctant to meet one-on-one with the professor.

Advice and Recommendations

Clearly a central feature of office hours is asking for and receiving advice. Therefore, it is important to recognize when you are getting advice and how strong that advice is. In Inter-action 1 on page 95, in response to the student's request for help, the instructor says, *Well, I would look at . . .* and *And I'd take a look at . . . .* Modal verbs *(may, might, can, could, would, should, must)* and quasi-modals *(need to, have to)* are important in making recommendations. The modal verbs moderate the strength of a recommendation.

Task 14

Discuss with a partner.

1. How do the two responses to the student questions differ?

   Student: What can I do to prepare for the exam?

   Instructor: Review the homework. *OR* I would review the homework.

   Student: Do you know where I can go to get some extra help on this paper?

   Instructor: Go to the writing center. *OR* You could go to the writing center.

2. Rank the following in terms of strongest (1) to weakest (6).

   _____ Maybe you should think about . . .

   _____ You had better . . . (You'd better . . .)

   _____ You could . . .

   _____ You might want to . . . (You might wanna . . .)

   _____ You should . . .

   _____ You need to . . .

   Would your rankings be the same regardless of whether the advice came from an instructor or a friend?

Maybe is often used to soften a *you* + (quasi)-MODAL construction. Without *maybe,* the advice or suggestion may sound a bit too direct or harsh. Compare these:

You should ask for more time.	*Maybe you should ask for more time.*
You need to get a calendar.	*Maybe you need to get a calendar.*

Alternatively, sometimes a question can soften the advice or suggestion:

You could get a tutor.	*Could you get a tutor?*
You should ask your lab partner.	*Should you ask your lab partner?*

And add *maybe* to the question for even greater effect:

> *Could you maybe get a tutor?*
>
> *Should you maybe ask your lab partner?*

Keep in mind that intonation is important for understanding the strength of any recommendation.

There are many ways that advice is given. Sometimes advice may be rather direct and strong. At other times, the advice may be rather indirect and weak. In the following tasks we'll look at some of the different ways that advice is given.

Task 15

Which of these do you think are the most common ways to give someone advice in an academic setting? Place a check (✔) in the corresponding blanks.

_____ I recommend . . .

_____ You might want to . . .

_____ You had better . . .

_____ I suggest that you . . .

_____ If I were you . . .

You may have thought that *suggest* and *recommend* would be the most common ways to offer advice as in,

> *I suggest/recommend that you talk to the professor.*

However, research on the MICASE database by John Swales and Sheryl Leicher indicates that *suggest* is rather infrequently used for this purpose. Below are some examples of *suggest/suggestion* as used to give advice.

> *I suggest (that) you start working on the paper soon.* (18 similar examples in MICASE)
>
> *What I would suggest is making an outline.* (19 similar examples in MICASE)
>
> *I'm suggesting (that) you think about taking another language.* (5 similar examples in MICASE)
>
> *My suggestion is to take a look at other resources.* (4 similar examples in MICASE)

Although it is possible to use *recommend,* it is also rather infrequently used. When it is used, it is more likely in the context of giving unsolicited advice, as in this office-hour interaction. Expressions used to give advice are in bold.

1. **Instructor:** You seriously interested in China?

2. **Student:** Yeah. I took the Chuang Tzu course last semester. Yeah. Chuang Tzu.

3. **Instructor:** Oh you did? Chuang Tzu? Oh, my favorite philosopher.

4. **Student:** Oh?

5. **Instructor:** He's the only religious writer that has good jokes.

6. **Student:** Yeah, he does.

7. **Instructor:** Anywhere. Uh in that case **let me recommend** a book, called *Bridge of Birds.* It's a fantasy novel. I use it in my, uh metaphors class. Freshman seminar. It's terrific.

8. **Student:** Okay.

(Based on MICASE. Linguistics Independent Study Advising, File ID: OFC355SU094)

Instructors also give unsolicited advice in their lectures, as in this example:

Instructor *<Lecturing>:* Uh coming back to, the comments on your papers, which I will hand out at the end of the class. Um, I think that it is really important for any graduate, any university graduate and certainly any graduate from the University of Michigan, to have good writing skills. I think that, um, one improves one's writing skills all through life. You know, it's not something where, a person takes a test and you know you can write, above some threshold and then sometime you stop. **Uh I, I always get people to read my drafts**, and they always, uh make improvements in, in the drafts. Because one of the things that happens is that you get so close to what you're working on that you, um, you sometimes lose perspective. **I really recommend** this. So, **I really recommend that** you, you think about this.

(Based on MICASE. Politics of Higher Education, File ID: SEM495SU111)

Because the words *recommend* and *suggest* are not used frequently, consider some other ways of giving advice, recommending, and suggesting. Questions are a more common way to give advice:

Why don't you . . . ?

Why don't you take another math class?

Why don't you go talk to your advisor?

Why don't we . . . ?

Why don't we take a break?

Why don't we take a look at this?

These question suggestions are rather straightforward and so it seems when you have a simple, direct suggestion, a question is a good option.

These questions are also possible, but they are not so common as advice-giving devices.

> How about/What about . . . ?
>
> *How about 2:15?*
>
> *How about meeting at 2:15?*
>
> What if we/What if you . . . ?
>
> *What if you looked at an old A paper and compared it to the paper that he gave you the D on?*

These kinds of questions tend to be more frequently used by an instructor to elicit student responses, as in

> *What if we increased the temperature?*
>
> *How about some other possible reasons?*

In MICASE, *let's* is not so common; however, it is a useful way to make a suggestion. Look at this interaction between a student and a professor.

> **Instructor:** Let's see I have a meeting tomorrow at 10:15. Um do you wanna meet before or after?
>
> **Student:** Either.
>
> **Instructor:** How m- how much time?
>
> **Student:** Just to discuss my assignment.
>
> **Instructor:** Um why don't we . . . . **Let's** say um two o'clock? Would that be okay? In my office?
>
> (Based on MICASE. Medical Anthropology Lecture, File ID: LEL115SU005)

When giving advice, advisors and instructors may be somewhat cautious for a variety of reasons. Perhaps the advice being given is rather burdensome or difficult to follow; perhaps your advisor or instructor is unsure of how you may react, or unsure of his or her own advice; perhaps the advisor or instructor wants to make it somewhat easy for you to reject the advice. In such cases, it is possible to use *might want* to or *might wanna,* which together are the most common way to give advice in MICASE. Consider the following examples in which *might want* to or *might wanna* are used to give advice.

Task 16

In the three interactions of office hours, a student has gone to the advisor or instructor for advice. Some of the language used to give advice is in bold. As you read the interaction, list in the chart any other expressions used to give advice. What kind of advice was the student looking for in each example? In your opinion, has the advisor or instructor been helpful or unhelpful?

	Expressions Used to Give Advice	**Kind of Advice Being Sought by Student**
Interaction 1	you might wanna	
Interaction 2	you might wanna	
Interaction 3	Well I wouldn't do that	

INTERACTION 1

1. **Advisor:** So, you're thinking about a political science class.
2. **Student:** Yeah I saw a course . . . like Introduction to World Politics or something [**Advisor:** Right] that, I uh . . .
3. **Advisor:** Which is Poli Sci 160.
4. **Student:** Okay. And then I was thinking maybe some science course.
5. **Advisor:** You know, **you might wanna** do that, and then **you might wanna** take, a biological anthro course or a beginning geology course or, [**Student:** Mhm] you know something like that, and then if you decide you wanna do geology or, bio anthro, then you could use that, poli sci for social science distribution. [**Student:** Right, okay] and if you decide you want some economics, then you take these other courses for natural science distribution.
6. **Student:** Right, okay.
7. **Advisor:** So nothing is wasted really.

(Based on MICASE. Honors Advising, File ID: ADV700JU023)

INTERACTION 2

1. **Advisor:** Well, a lot of professors think you should do all of the assigned problems not once, but three times. So, they're encouraging you to be obsessive.
2. **Student:** Oh wow. What do you mean like all the assigned problems? You mean like all the homeworks?
3. **Advisor:** All of the homework. Mhm.

4. **Student:** So, every time you do homework you should do it three times?

5. **Advisor:** Yeah but not necessarily three times in a row. First [**Student:** Oh] You know first you read the chapters in your textbook as they're assigned but don't stop there. Then you do the problem sets at the end of each section right after you've read it . . . right? Cuz then you know right off the bat that, if you can do all the problems, you're confident that you know it. [**Student:** Mhm] If right after you've gotten the reading, you do the problems and you find yourself pulling your hair out, you know at a fairly early point in the term, that all is not well. And at that point to get, you know . . . go talk to your friends, go talk to your instructor, go bother people. <*laugh*> Do it before you move on to another topic. <*laugh*> And you, you need to say to yourself okay I need to go back to the beginning and figure out what topics I've, I've missed. [**Student:** Mhm] This and this is probably something that you should do, with the stuff. It's got to be done pretty consistently. Cuz I don't think you should try to go back and redo it all at one time cuz that's cramming. And I don't think people learn real well that way. [**Student:** Right no] But if you could do like a little bit of an old homework assignment.

6. **Student:** Like at the end of each like at the end of each week just do all the homework from the week?

7. **Advisor:** Right and since you missed some stuff **you might wanna** do all the homework from the week but then go back and review, <*laugh*> [**Student:** Yeah] something that you didn't understand. [**Student:** Right]

(Based on MICASE. Academic Advising, File ID: ADV700JU047)

INTERACTION 3

1. **Instructor:** Now, if you look at this graph, you can see that there are all kinds of values that you can pick from for the calculation. The highest, seems to be . . . 1.02

2. **Student:** Yeah.

3. **Instructor:** Okay, so 1.02 is the highest one and the lowest one goes to .063. So, which one would you choose, to do your calculation?

4. **Student:** The average, the average of them.

5. **Instructor:** The average? <*laugh*> **Well, I wouldn't do that**.

6. **Student:** What do you mean?

7. **Instructor:** . . . well what would I do then? Well do you have any other idea?

8. **Student:** What about this point here? Where there is a steady . . . .

9. **Instructor:** Huh?

10. **Student:** Could you use that or not?

11. **Instructor:** You could do that, but you have to consider these other factors. For example, . . .

(Based on MICASE. Hydraulics Problem Solving Lab, File ID: LAB205SU045)

Accepting and Rejecting Advice, Recommendations, or Suggestions

Once you have received a piece of advice, you should acknowledge it and then decide whether to accept or reject it. Generally, acknowledging the advice can be something as simple as *okay, alright,* or maybe even *yes* (see examples in bold in Interactions 1 and 2). After acknowledging the advice, speakers often will comment on it or indicate whether they will take it or not, as in these examples.

Task 17

Read these interactions. Then answer the questions.

INTERACTION 1

1. **Instructor:** Well, I'd say overall the paper is okay. But there are a few things you could do to improve it a bit.
2. **Student:** Uh huh.
3. **Instructor:** For example, you might wanna move your definition of sustainable up. I think it's coming too late in the paper.
4. **Student: Uh okay**. Like where, though. I don't see a good place for it.
5. **Instructor:** You could place it here. After food shortages.
6. **Student: Alright**. Yeah I see. It would fit there wouldn't it? How about if I put it here?
7. **Instructor:** Yeah, that . . . would work.

INTERACTION 2

1. **Advisor:** Have you thought about moving? I mean if your roommate is so inconsiderate and all.
2. **Student: Yeah.** But if I move, then I'll miss all my friends.
3. **Advisor:** But you say your roommate is impossible. Who has to have the TV on all night? It's so . . . a little unusual.
4. **Student:** I know, but it's not that easy. I don't know.
5. **Advisor:** So, if you want to stay, then you have to try to make it . . . make it work. Talk to your roommate and say just what you said to me.
6. **Student: Okay,** uh yeah. Uh huh.

How likely is it that the student will indeed talk to the roommate? In other words, how strong is the acceptance of the advice?

Sometimes you may not want to accept the advice you are given, as in this interaction between an advisor and a graduate student.

INTERACTION 3

1. **Advisor:** So, what can I do for you?
2. **Student:** I need to talk about my schedule next semester.
3. **Advisor:** When are you taking your qualifying exams for your PhD?
4. **Student:** Next spring.
5. **Advisor:** Have you thought about Econ 620?
6. **Student:** Uh. No not really. I'm not really . . . .
7. **Advisor:** Ready for it? You've taken 520 haven't you? So you're ready.
8. **Student: Yes, but** I uh. **I don't** uh . . .
9. **Advisor:** I think you should. Especially if you're going to take your exams.
10. **Student: Yes, but** . . .

The student really does not want to take Econ 620. What should he/she say next?

Pronunciation Focus: /T/

Introduction

One factor influencing how a word is pronounced is the sounds that immediately precede or follow the word. It's also important to consider that, unlike in writing where each word is visually separate from all other words, in speaking, words and sounds are nearly always connected to create a fairly continuous stream of sounds within word or thought groups. Thus, when two words are said in succession, the boundary between those words may not necessarily be clear. Another result of this continuous stream of speech is that word initial and word final sounds may be pronounced differently from how they are spoken in isolation.

Take a look at this sentence.

I'm having a problem with the homework. I just can't figure it out.

In this sentence, /t/ is not pronounced in the same way in all instances. The /t/ in *just* and *can't* may actually not be said at all; the /t/ in *it* will likely be pronounced as a /d/. (Note that this phenomenon in which a /t/ is pronounced like a /d/ also occurs within words such as *water* or *matter*.)

In this focus section we look at how /t/ is pronounced in context. How will the /t/ likely be pronounced in each of these sentences?

1. I have a lot of reading for this class.
2. I forgot all of my books this morning.
3. The test is on Monday.
4. What are you doing this weekend?
5. I should go to a review session.

Data Collection and Analysis

Part 1: Transcription

With one or two partners, listen to Unit 4, Office Hour Concerns, Scene 2 on the DVD, and then choose one to two minutes of speech to transcribe. Each of you should transcribe what you hear, listening to the DVD as many times as you need. You can listen together or individually. Once everyone is done transcribing, compare your transcriptions and try to create a complete transcript of the section you chose. Listen to the DVD again if necessary. Indicate any places in the recording where you cannot figure out what is being said and ask your instructor for some assistance.

Part 2: Analysis

With your partners, mark the instances of /t/ in your transcript and note how they are pronounced.

Part 3: Report to the class

Your report should provide the following information:

1. Remind your listeners of the focus of your investigation.
2. What, if anything, made it difficult to identify the instances of /t/? Was it the surrounding words? The recording? The speakers' rates of speaking? Characteristics of the speakers' pronunciations?
3. What are your group's observations on how /t/ is pronounced? What, if any, other interesting pronunciation observations did your group make?

Part 4: Production

With a partner, read aloud and/or role-play your transcript, paying special attention to your pronunciation of /t/ in context.

UNIT 5

Classroom Interactions

In this unit we will take a close look at class participation and classroom interactions. In many classes in U.S. colleges and universities, instructors often state that they want students to participate in class and that they will factor participation into final course grades.

Class participation poses a number of challenges for both instructors and students. One main challenge is that instructors and students often have different ideas of what it means to participate in class. For some students, particularly those who tend to talk in class, class participation means making a verbal contribution. Quiet students, however, tend to view participation more broadly to include attending class, being prepared, listening, and doing all of the homework (Fritschner 2000). For instructors, what constitutes class participation depends on the type of class. In large introductory survey courses, just coming to class and paying attention might be viewed as a form of class participation. However, in smaller classes, students are expected to verbally contribute on a regular basis.

Although professors say that they value student contributions in class, research has shown that most students do not participate. According to Crombie et al. (2003), on average, a small number of students do the vast majority of speaking in class: typically four or five students are responsible for 75 percent of all the interactions in classes of 40 or fewer students. This phenomenon is known as the consolidation of responsibility, in which just a few students speak in class, while the rest of the students remain silent. A further factor in class participation is that professors do almost 80 percent of the talking in a typical class (Weaver and Qi 2005). It's no wonder then that students may have trouble speaking in class.

Some students are very eager to participate in class, while others would prefer to simply be passive observers, not saying a word. What is your preference?

We'll begin by looking at attitudes both students and instructors have toward class participation, and then look at how to participate and ask questions. Near the end of the unit we also consider the role of storytelling (personal narratives) in an academic course.

By the end of this unit you should be able to

- understand why students do or do not participate in class
- have some strategies for participating in class
- pose questions in a variety of ways
- have strategies for understanding ellipsis in speaking.

Task 1

Discuss these questions with a partner.

1. What is class participation, in your opinion?

2. How frequently do you talk in class? Do you volunteer or do you talk only if called upon?

3. Do you sometimes wish you had said something in a class? What prevented you? What other factors might prevent students from talking in class?

4. What factors do you think promote student participation in class?

5. How important do you think it is for you to talk in class? When students do talk in class, do they say anything important or interesting?

6. If you are familiar with classroom interaction styles (university or other level) in another country, discuss whether students are expected to participate in classes in that country. Are the relationships of students and instructors in that country different from those in the United States?

7. Research suggests that a student's level of interaction with an instructor outside of class (e.g., office hour visits) influences his or her level of class participation. Why do you think this is the case?

In general, instructors at U.S. colleges and universities expect students to demonstrate more individual initiative and be more involved in daily class activities than may be expected in universities outside the United States (Baron 1975). Because of prior experience in another country, some students may also expect more formal relationships with their professors than most American students would. In addition to this, some students may think it is impolite to ask questions or give opinions in class. Thus the classroom atmosphere, including the type and degree of faculty-student interaction in American colleges and universities, may be problematic (Craig 1981; Edwards and Tonkin 1990).

Some instructors want students to raise their hands before speaking in class, and this of course is a very common way to have an opportunity to talk, as demonstrated by these excerpts.

Task 2

Read these excerpts regarding class participation, and discuss the questions with a partner.

EXCERPT 1

Instructor A: And also, maybe I should emphasize that you should try and interrupt me, if you're, during the lecture if you're if you're um, if there're some points of unclarity. Just jump in an- and you know yell, and let me know.

(Based on MICASE. First Year Philosophy Seminar, File ID: SEM475JU084)

EXCERPT 2

Instructor B: Now don't be alarmed by some of the, some of the mathematics that's going to come. It's all incredibly simple and if you need an explanation just ask me. Stop me and I'll explain.

(Based on MICASE. Problem Solving Colloquium, File ID: COL999MX059)

EXCERPT 3

Instructor C: We move so fast and so, I just if you're feeling uncertain about things, you'll get certain with them really quite quickly. Um, I want to encourage you again to stop and ask whenever, you don't understand, or, need some clarification or whatever of anything I'm saying or, uh because, it's very hard to know what you don't get, unless you ask us, so I really encourage you to do that.

(Based on MICASE. Statistics in Social Sciences Lecture, File ID: LES565MX152)

EXCERPT 4

Instructor D: One consideration that's very important *<pause:04>* is schemas. What are schemas? *<pause:10>* We can describe schemas as ways of looking at the world *<pause:06>* prototypes *<pause:04>* schemas have been defined all sorts of different ways. Ways of looking at the world prototypes models, you know, what we define as, typical. What's typical? So a very common schema exercise, is if I say to you describe a chair. Tell me what a chair has. How do you describe a chair? What has it got? What features does it have? Just shout 'em out.

(Based on MICASE. Media Impact in Communication Lecture, File ID: LEL220SU073)

EXCERPT 5

Instructor E: I hope that lecture can be at least a modest amount of back and forth. If you have questions please, raise your hands, um right away. Don't just, uh listen to me and scribble down everything I say it's it's likely to be wrong or many times it could be wrong, or sometimes I'll just say things to be provocative. Um, or if I have an opinion, it's just my opinion and in that case can be challenged, just as much as anybody else's opinion. . . . The point of this is, and I've seen it in many great lecture halls, big lecture halls, is that, the heads just bob up and down in tune with what the professor is scribbling and nobody ever asks a question. So, um, don't let me get away with something you disagree with. Challenge me uh challenge all your professors, but definitely make it interactive. And if you don't, I'm gonna start calling on people, and when when I figure out some of your names then you're definitely fair game.

(Based on MICASE. Intro Biology First Day Lecture, File ID: LEL175MU014)

1. In Excerpts 1–4, what do the instructors want their students to do if they want to ask a question or get clarification in class?

2. Why does the instructor in Excerpt 5 want students to participate in class?

3. In Excerpt 5, what does *back and forth* mean? What does *scribbling* mean? What does *heads just bob up and down* mean?

4. What does the instructor in Excerpt 5 mean when he/she says, *So, um, don't let me get away with something you disagree with*?

5. What will the instructor in Excerpt 5 do if students do not voluntarily participate? Do you think this is fair? Would you be comfortable with this?

6. What does the instructor in Excerpt 5 mean about students being *fair game*?

7. Would you feel comfortable disagreeing with (challenging) your instructors as the instructor in Excerpt 5 advises students to?

Questions and Answers

Student Questions

In Unit 2, we looked at questions as part of an interview, but in this unit we discuss questions in a classroom setting. We saw how students might respond to an instructor's question with a question to show uncertainty about their answers. But often students will have to ask questions because they don't understand or they need to clarify something an instructor said. Being able to ask questions appropriately will give you confidence to participate in classroom interactions.

These examples illustrate how students can ask questions. The relevant phrases have been bolded for you.

1. *I don't see*

   I don't see how that works.

2. *how come*

   How come that won't work?

3. Tags: *right, isn't it, and so on*

   That's what we need to study for the exam, **right**?

   That material is in chapter one, **isn't it**?

4. *Wait / wait a minute*

   Instructor: So, we should increase taxes to make up for the loss. It would just be a small increase and people shouldn't mind paying a bit more. Cuz in the end, people want to have the services. People won't mind an extra $20 or so because they . . . .

   Student: Wait wait a minute. Wait you lost me there. What are you saying? Are you making a philosophical point? Or are you telling us that you know a small increase in taxes doesn't matter to most people?

   Instructor: The homework this week is due on Monday not Wednesday.

   Student: Wait wait. How are we gonna get it to you? There's no class on Monday cuz of the break.

Student Comments

These expressions are useful if a student wants to participate by commenting on something the instructor or another student has said. Notice one of these phrases (in bold) is used in the next excerpt and that it is preceded by the word *um*. Why do you suppose Student 4 said *um* before speaking?

> I wanted to say . . .
>
> I just wanna say . . .
>
> I was just gonna say . . .

Instructor: We we fear what we don't know, right? So there were the communists and here there were the little political ads. You saw the Johnson ad where . . . you had the little girl and the suggestion that she's being blown up by a nuclear bomb? Right? There's a lot of fear. How much information do you think your average American had about what communism was?

Student 1: A little.

Student 2: Very little.

Student 3: Just that it was bad.

Instructor: Just that it was bad? Yeah. That it was different from us? Yeah. Katy?

Student 4: Um, I was just gonna say um that people do, fear what they don't understand and our lack of knowledge . . . of all of these different cultures. Different, you know, styles of doing things lead us to believe that ours is the right way and the best way to do something.

Instructor: OK, uh right. So, Angie?

(Based on MICASE. Politics Discussion Section, File ID: DIS495JU119)

Instructor Questions

Questions from instructors feature prominently in many of the MICASE transcripts of classroom interactions. The purpose of the questions varies. Some questions are meant to be answered by the students; others are not.

Instructors often use non-threatening questions and rhetorical questions in their classes. Non-threatening questions are intended to encourage students to participate. Given this goal, a non-threatening question may ask something very obvious, ask students to guess or speculate, or push students to think about a topic. To encourage learning, instructors may ask a series of questions with each successive question based on a student response.

A rhetorical question, on the other hand, is a question to which the speaker expects no answer but is asked anyway to have an effect on the listener, such as to get the listener interested in a topic. Rhetorical questions may also be used to make a transition to a new topic. In some cases, a rhetorical question may be posed to give the appearance of being interested in what a listener has understood. For instance, an instructor may ask, *Are there any questions?* even though he or she does not really want or expect questions.

Task 3

Underline the questions in these lecture examples. Then discuss Questions 1 and 2.

CLASS A

Instructor: Uh before we move on to the government response to higher milk prices, are there any questions about the reasons that milk has become so expensive these days? Okay. Well what I'd like to do first . . . is review the possible ways that government can influence the price of something like milk. We did briefly go through some general responses yesterday but I think this is uh tough enough to understand that we probably oughta go through it, uh, quicker this time but go through it again, and then when we look at specific options this may be a bit more clear.

(Based on MICASE. Intro Programming Lecture, File ID: LES235SU099)

CLASS B

Instructor: We can have very different approaches to agriculture . . . one type of agriculture, sometimes called horticulture, is known as shifting cultivation, that means that, you have a community, that, will will um farm some land for a period of time. But after time, the soil becomes depleted, of whatever it is, of the resources needed, nutrients needed for that particular crop. So what will happen when the soil is depleted? Well, after a period of time, people will leave that plot alone, and move on, and start another, plot with the same crop. And then they, they're just . . . moving around shifting cultivation.

(Based on MICASE. Intro Anthropology Lecture, File ID: LEL115JU090)

1. Can you tell whether the instructors did or did not want (or expect) anyone to respond to the questions? How?

2. Imagine you are a student in Class A. What would you do if you really did have a question about why milk prices are higher? What are the advantages and disadvantages of each of these possibilities?
   a. Interrupt the instructor and ask your question.
   b. Ask another student.
   c. Forget about your question, assuming it probably does not matter.
   d. Email the instructor with your question.
   e. Go to the instructor's office hours to ask your question.

If you wanted to interrupt the professor to ask your question, what would you say? Check MICASE to look for examples of interrupting. Work with a partner to come up with expressions that you could search for.

In Class A, the instructor is likely too impatient to wait for questions and has merely asked a question in order to appear to be concerned about the students' understanding; in Class B, however, the intent of the question is different. While the instructor in B does not necessarily expect an answer to this rhetorical question, the question does have the effect of letting the students very briefly think about the effect of soil depletion and providing an introduction to the next point.

Task 4

Read this excerpt from a Biology lecture, and discuss the questions with your partner.

1. **Instructor:** You know what a filter feeder is? I bet you can imagine. Take a guess. What do you think . . . ?

2. **Rebecca:** Sediments . . . something like . . . bottom feeders? *<with rising intonation>*

3. **Instructor:** Yeah, Rebecca, the- they're nonselective, eaters. It's like my son. Anything that comes by 'em, . . . they eat it. Now there're all sorts of filter feeders. Rebecca talked about the bottom, filter feeders, which just go in, and just eat mud. Anything that's in the mud, that they can digest digest it . . . .

4. **John:** Are these, like . . . when I was reading today . . . it was saying something to that extent, but wouldn't it also be kinda like, they get a lot of these particles, and what if they ate other things or something? . . . it wouldn't be . . . it wouldn't necessarily be a filter feeder. But what if another fish ate another fish?

5. **Instructor:** Oh yeah, you can, you can send it up the food chain, for sure. But down, right above the plants, which . . . which are, the base of the food chain . . . there are a lot of small . . . organisms, who do nothing but, rake through the ocean with these, arms with little hairs on 'em, and grab anything that's there. Anything at all. And it's just like the bottom feeders that Rebecca, mentioned, they ingest it.

(Based on MICASE. Intro Oceanography Lecture, File ID: LEL305JU092)

1. Read the instructor's questions in Turn 1. How confident is he/she that the students might have an answer?

2. How likely would you be to respond to the instructor's question? Why?

3. How does Rebecca respond to the instructor's question? How confident is she? How can you tell?

4. How does the instructor respond to Rebecca's answer? Does the instructor seem supportive of the student's effort to say something? Why?

5. How do you think the instructor might have responded if the student had given an answer that was completely incorrect?

6. How confident does John seem in his comment? Does the instructor's answer seem supportive of him?

7. Why does the instructor mention his son? Many American instructors do reveal a bit about themselves or their families in class. Does getting some of this personal information influence your attitude toward an instructor?

If an instructor is encouraging students to participate, as in the excerpt, almost any reasonable response will be met positively, even one that is tentative, uncertain, or perhaps wrong. In the excerpt, Rebecca shows her uncertainty by hedging her answer in two ways. First, she says *something like* and then uses a question or rising intonation. Essentially, the student has answered the instructor's question with a question.

Hedging a Response

A hedge is a word or expression that modifies something you are saying. Hedges have specific communicative purposes, such as to convey politeness, vagueness, or uncertainty. Hedges can also be used to lessen the severity of or mitigate what you say. For instance, if, like Rebecca, you want to respond to a question but are not sure if you have the right answer, you can hedge your answer by responding with a question. Apart from using simple rising intonation, there are other ways to hedge a response to a question asking for some factual information.

For example, hedged responses to the question *What is a filter feeder?* might be:

1. a yes-no question

   Is it (maybe) a bottom feeder?

2. an expression of a lack of knowledge

   I don't know. Maybe a bottom feeder.

3. a guess with a modal verb

   It could be a bottom feeder.

   I would guess/say a bottom feeder.

In addition to answering a specific content question, you might need to respond to questions that ask your opinion. When offering opinions, speakers often use hedges to either soften their ideas or to express some uncertainty.

Read these examples of some commonly used hedges.

1. modal verbs: *may, might, could*

    That **may be** true.

    If tuition increases, some students **might not be** able to afford to go to school.

    I think this material **could be** on the exam.

2. *kind of*—somewhat, to some extent.

    The lecture was **kind of** interesting.

    Compare to *kind* meaning "type," which is not used as a hedge.

    This **kind of** weather will be hard on plants.

3. *sort of*—somewhat, to some extent

    I **sort of** agree.

    Compare to *sort* meaning "type," which is not used as a hedge.

    You need some **sort of** system that is not very expensive.

4. *generally, generally speaking, in general*

    This class **generally** has a lot of homework.

    Generally speaking, the homework is easier than the exams.

    In general, there are two ways to solve this problem.

5. *usually*

    I **usually** study in the library.

6. *really*

    Really when used after the verb has a softening effect.

    I don't **really** enjoy psychology class.

    Compare to using *really* before the verb, which serves to strengthen the point.

    I **really** don't enjoy my psychology class.

7. *maybe*

    I was thinking **maybe** I should take a math class.

8. *I guess*

> **I guess** my point is that students need more financial support.

9. *just wanted*

> I **just wanted** to point out that there are a few ways to solve these problems.

To check how common these hedges are, go to MICASE, and search for the words or phrases in bold. Can you think of any other hedges? Check for them in the MICASE corpus as well.

Task 5

Read this classroom interaction between the instructor and students, and underline the language used to adjust the strength of the opinions being offered. Note also how the instructor keeps asking questions to encourage students to offer a suggestion. The class is discussing how to increase the level of sales of a company that sells prepared foods such as breakfast cereal.

1. **Instructor:** Alright, can I get your attention please? . . . So what sorts of ideas have you come up with what sorts of uh, what sorts of things might, might Brenda Cooper do as the regional manager to reconfigure the the reward system? To get salespeople to sell more. Whatta you think, whatta you think she might do? Kirk?

2. **Kirk:** Um well, I guess instead of basing, um your salary, on how you do compared to the plan, they might wanna base salary on a percent, of your sales. So, that gives you more incentive to, to, keep, selling, um, . . . it's you know there's a positive reinforcement.

3. **Instructor:** Okay so you're not punished for, increasing the quota. But, you're in fact rewarded for it. Other ideas? Mike?

4. **Mike:** We kind of like thought that you should think in the short term, and then in the long term. Like, in the long term there's a lot of better alternatives . . . you know, stock options. But in the short term . . . they could think about rewarding the entire sales region. Therefore they might have better sales and one district might be more prone to like, share their ideas because if someone's not working hard in their district then, they're gonna actually be hurt. It may have a negative side, but I would think as a whole it might, stimulate sales.

5. **Instructor:** And how would you do that? Any of the groups have thoughts about how you would do that? H- how might you do it? How might you, do that so you get the whole region . . . you reward performance in the whole region? Any, any thoughts about how you might do that? Kurt?

6. **Kurt:** You could have little bonuses for the whole region instead of specific districts. Say the whole, region meets their sales quota then, everybody in the region gets a bonus, but if the region doesn't meet the sales goal, then nobody gets a bonus.

7. **Instructor:** So therefore, if my district figures out, that there's a market for baby food among the elderly, maybe we won't keep that information to ourselves because if the whole region increases in sales, we get a bigger bonus. Other thoughts? What else might you do for the bonus system? Good, Jessica?

8. **Jessica:** Centralize the paperwork? Then they could sell more, without feeling that they were spending more time selling. Because the sales force said oh we have to do the paperwork so we can't sell. Well, if paperwork is centralized, they'd spend less time on paperwork and more time selling. They'd be working the same amount of time but could still sell more, and could get a bonus also.

9. **Instructor:** Okay, that's another approach. Anyone else? Jessica?

10. **Jessica:** I just wanted to ask if . . . well uh maybe you could have another kind of reward that isn't connected uh uh connected to money? I mean, what if you offered to upgrade office space when the sales goals are met? You know, make the environment better. Like have a really amazing space where people could have lunch and relax.

(Based on MICASE. Behavior Theory Management Lecture, File ID: LEL185SU066)

You might have noticed that the instructor in this classroom interaction asks a lot of questions. Questions clearly encourage students to participate, especially when they are directed to a specific student. Besides encouraging students to talk, questions have another purpose. Questions allow an instructor to determine what the students do and do not know, which may then cause the instructor to adjust the content of the lesson. Questions also reveal the extent to which the class is understanding and whether the students can apply concepts that have been introduced. Finally, questions may also encourage the students to think during class, rather than being passive absorbers of information.

Task 6

Read this excerpt from another Biology lecture. The class is discussing how plants survive. Underline each of the instructor's questions, and decide the purpose of each. Is the purpose to check prior knowledge? To check understanding of lecture content? To encourage thinking? With your partner, discuss the questions.

1. **Instructor**: Right next to your house, is a very common place, for trees to start to grow, ironically enough, and why is that? *<pause: 8 seconds>* Anybody have an idea, why trees start to grow, spontaneously right where we don't want them?

2. **Jonathan:** Is it because there's more shelter right next to a house?

3. **Instructor:** Sounds like a good idea. Can you explain?

4. **Jonathan:** Is it because there's more shelter, for the seeds?

5. **Instructor:** Let's think for a second. Is there more shelter of a very special kind? *<pause: 9 seconds>*

6. **Jonathan:** Is it protection from the wind?

7. **Instructor:** Perhaps a little protection of the wind, but I have something else in mind. What's out there in your yard that might not be good for a tree?

8. **Lauren:** Protection from lawn mowers?

9. **Instructor:** Protection from your . . . , Lauren?

10. **Lauren:** Lawn mower.

11. **Instructor:** Lawn mower. Yes, protection from your lawn mower. Tree seedlings, really, don't like, to be mown. And in fact, what keeps your lawn a lawn, and not, a forest, is because you mow it. If you didn't mow your lawn, and you looked at it in twenty years, it'd be covered with trees. That's because we live in an eastern hardwood forest, where the potential vegetation is a hardwood forest. That means if we stop doing anything, and let nature take its course, it ultimately reverts back to, goes back to, the eastern hardwood forest.

(Based on MICASE. Practical Botany Lecture, File ID: LEL175JU086)

1. Why do you suppose the instructor is asking so many questions?

2. Are the questions in Turn 1 directed at a particular student? How can you tell?

3. Do you think the students needed to raise their hands to answer?

4. How does the instructor attempt to draw out answers from the students?

5. How does the instructor react to the answers that are not quite right?

6. What do you think is the effect of this kind of response on the students? How comfortable are the students responding to questions?

7. In Turn 1 the instructor waits eight seconds before repeating his questions. In Turn 5, there is another pause of nine seconds. Why? What is the effect of pauses or wait time?

8. Can you identify any instances of hedging?

Wh-Clefts

In Excerpt (Class) A in Task 3 on page 125, the instructor uses a very common construction to preview the focus of the day's class.

> Uh before we move on to the government response to higher milk prices, are there any questions about the reasons that milk has become so expensive these days? Okay. <u>well what I'd like to do first . . . is</u> review the possible ways that government can influence the price of something like milk.

The underlined structure is known as a *wh*-cleft. **Clefts** are used to focus on an important element of a sentence. *Wh*-cleft sentences consist of these parts.

- *Wh*-clause + *is/are* + noun phrase, a nominal clause, or an infinitive clause

In such sentences, the primary focus is on the end of the sentence.

You can use *wh*-clefts for questions or statements.

> What I wanted to ask about is the reasons prices are increasing.

> What he was explaining was the factors preventing an easy solution.

Task 7

Read this excerpt from a discussion in a class on politics of higher education, and underline all the *wh*-clefts.

1. **Instructor:** OK. Let's talk about the papers for this week. Jeremy, why don't you start and, tell us what your, thoughts were about this.

2. **Jeremy:** Um, what I focused on, I'm trying to remember what *<laugh>*, was that distance learning, and uh about these virtual universities, are basically not giving someone the same education. And, uh, what I wrote about is there are drawbacks to distance learning and, I don't have a hard copy here because my, my printer's broken, but uh . . . .

3. **Instructor:** So what are the drawbacks?

4. **Jeremy:** Well, what the main drawback of distance learning is the uh, that you, lose out on the experience of um the me- maturation process which occurs from, sitting in classrooms even if you're a commuting student. Um, from having, you know the professor, in front of the room saying this is due on Tuesday or whatever. Being in the class-

room forces you to think uh, it it makes it more concrete, as opposed to if you see it online.

5. **Instructor:** What if I just show a video?

6. **Jeremy:** If you're in the classroom setting still with other students, it's uh, there's still the the academia feeling, and uh, [**Instructor:** It's a different feeling] right. And uh, specifically with going away to school there there's such a change that students go through. If someone was to, um, do their courses online they wouldn't be able to experience the change overall as a person that one gains from going away to school. Um, but I did write about that I, recognized the fact that there are people who can't go away to um, I forget specifically what I wrote about I I went into more detail and I cited some stuff but it's been a while since I, <**Instructor:** *laugh*> read my own my own piece <*laugh*>. But, what you need to think about is that there is an interaction part of the class that's important.

7. **Instructor:** OK. Yeah, that's good. Who else wants to contribute besides Jeremy? Aw, c'mon who else? Everybody else in here. Somebody must be missing because I think I had uh <*pause:06 sec*> let's see, is uh, let's see . . . Stephanie.

8. **Stephanie:** OK, yeah . . . . What Jeremy just said makes sense. I mean we couldn't have this same discussion in an online course, could we? . . .

(Based on MICASE. Politics of Higher Education, File ID: SEM495SU111)

Task 8

Choose the *wh*-clauses that can reasonably complete the sentences in the transcript. For some sentences, more than one *wh*-clause will work.

What I mean is   What it seems like to me is   What I've noticed looking back
                                                           at my last few years here is

What I'm saying is   What you need to do is

1. **Instructor:** What do you know about, other cultures? Did anyone encounter new cultures when they came to Michigan?

2. **S1:** Yes

3. **S2:** Yeah

4. **Instructor:** And so what do you do with that new information? John?

5. **S1:** Well um (1) _____that lot of people know only superficial things about other cultures. [**Instructor:** Mhm] It's based on what they see other people doing or what they hear through media or through, school or through their family. But if you don't, if you don't live, like that culture lives or like that race lives or, that religion then, you're not gonna see you're not gonna understand what, goes on in, in that culture . . . .

6. **Instructor:** Do we tend to have real nice things to say about people who are different than us? [**S2**: No] just generally speaking? What do you think? We as Americans do we generally have nice things to say about people who are not like us?

7. **S2:** (2)_____ is that people do all sorts of things, (3) _____ that we can't make a broad-based generalization like that.

8. **Instructor:** You don't think so? [**S2:** I don't think so] How's that?

9. **S2:** *<laugh>* I, I just don't think we can. (4) _____ that America is made up of many different types of people and some people are very accepting and others aren't, and, that's reality. And so some people have nice things to say or even if they don't have nice things they don't know enough. But I I don't think that you, I don't think that you could classify it. (5) _____ you should do a survey about how people feel about the people that are different.

(Based on MICASE. Intro to American Politics Discussion Section, File ID: DIS495JU119)

Task 9

Go to the MICASE website, and look for examples of *wh*-clefts. You can begin by looking for one of these expressions:

> What I think was/is . . .

> What I found was . . .

Ellipsis

As mentioned in Unit 1, page 16, the word *ellipsis* comes from Greek, meaning "falling short," and is the term used to describe the omission of a portion of a phrase or a sentence.

You may have already noticed in many of the transcripts in this unit that speakers are not always using complete sentences. For example, in the transcript in Task 5, the instructor says:

Instructor: Okay so you're not punished for, increasing the quota. But, you're in fact rewarded for it. Other ideas? Mike?

Instructor: Any, any thoughts about how you might do that? Kurt?

We can also find examples of ellipsis in the transcript in Task 6.

Instructor: Sounds like a good idea. Can you explain?

Ellipsis is quite common in spoken, unrehearsed speech. It's important to know that speakers frequently omit parts of sentences so that you don't think that you have somehow missed something.

Look at these examples of responses with ellipsis followed by the same example in its full form. Some uses of ellipsis are fairly easy to understand, like these first few examples.

A: Is the exam on Thursday?
B: [with ellipsis] No, Monday.

    [full form]   No, the exam is on Monday.

A: Where can I get the book?
B: [with ellipsis] The Campus Book Store. Probably the bookstore at the union, too.

    [full form]   You can get it at the Campus Book store. Probably the bookstore at the Union has it too.

    or   The Campus Book store has it. It is probably at the bookstore at the union, too.

Look at these sentences that include a *wh*-word. What is missing?

A: The instructor said something about tomorrow's homework, but I don't know what.
B: We're supposed to have a quiz soon, but I don't know when.

In Sentence A, *he said* is missing after the *wh*-word; in Sentence B, *it is* is missing.

There are many situations where words or phrases can be omitted. Some common kinds of ellipsis involving the subject and verb in declarative sentences and questions follow.

Declarative Sentences

In declarative sentences, ellipsis often involves the omission of *I*, *it*, *that,* and *there* in subject position. It also involves the omission of the verb *to be* and occasionally the verb *have.*

Omission of the Subject in Declarative Sentences

Omission of *I*

A: Your advisor's looking for you.
B: Wonder what she wants.

A: What time's the talk?
B: Don't know.
    (Dunno.)

A: Thanks for the help.
B: Hope you'll do OK.

Omission of *it* or *that*

> **A:** What do you think about the start of my paper?
> **B:** Looks pretty good.

> **A:** Could we meet at 10:00.
> **B:** Sounds fine.

> **A:** How'd you do on the test? I didn't do so well.
> **B:** Me either.* Seems like no matter how much I study, I don't do well.
>   (* You might also hear *me neither.*)

Omission of *there, there is,* or *there are*

> **A:** I didn't get all the points for this problem.
> **B:** Could be a mistake. Let's see.

> **A:** Do we have a test some time soon?
> **B:** Should be one next week, I think.

> **A:** Do we have homework this week?
> **B:** Not much. Just a few problems in the book.

Omission of the Subject and Verb in Declarative Sentences

Omission of *I* + *be*

> **A:** Where've you been?
> **B:** Sorry to be late.

> **A:** We need to leave. It's almost time for class.
> **B:** OK. Coming.

> **A:** Have you ever heard of Andrew Wyeth?
> **B:** Not sure. Is he an artist?

Omission of *it* + *be*

> **A:** Good morning. Beautiful day, isn't it.
> **B:** Hi. Good to see you.
>   (Notice that the article *a* before *beautiful* is also missing.)

> **A:** Class was cancelled this morning.
> **B:** No wonder no one else was there. I didn't know.

> **A:** I enjoyed talking to you.
> **B:** Yeah, nice talking to you, too.

Omissions in Questions

Omission of *be*

A: You okay?
B: Yeah. Just a bit tired.

A: She coming to class today?
B: Not sure, but I would think so.

A: Everything clear at this point?
B: Yeah.

Omission of *there + be*

A: Any more questions?
B: Yeah. I was wondering when the quiz is.

A: Questions or problems?
B: No. I think it's okay.

Omission of *you + be*

A: Working late?
B: Yeah. I've got a lot of homework.

A: Still working on your paper?
B: No, I actually finished it yesterday.

A: Going to class?
B: Yeah, and I'm probably gonna be late.

Omission of *do* in questions with *you*

A: You follow me?
B: Yeah, everything's clear.

A: You speak Japanese?
B: A little.

A: You like your classes this semester?
B: Yeah, pretty much.

Omission of *you + do*

A: Want to come?
   (Wanna come?)
B: Sure.

A: Need some help?
B: Yeah, a little.

A: Got a minute?
   (Gotta minute?)
B: Sure. What's up?

Task 10

Read these short examples and, in the blank, write the elements, if any, that have been omitted.

A: Going to the game this weekend?   _____

B: Depends on the weather.   _____

A: Same with me.   _____

A: You going to the lecture this afternoon?   _____

B: Probably. It sounds interesting.   _____

A: Yeah, might be kind of interesting.   _____

A: You okay?   _____

B: Yeah, just a bit tired.   _____

A: It's been a tough week. Too much homework. _____

B: No doubt about it.   _____

Task 11

In the examples written in complete sentences, rewrite the conversation, omitting elements where possible to produce sentences with ellipsis. Remember that not every turn will have ellipsis. After you are done, read the two versions of the conversation with a partner. Does one of the two sound more natural to you than the other?

Conversation Full Sentences	Ellipsis
A: Are you going to math class?	
B: Yes, I am going. Are you going?	
A: I am probably not going. I have to finish my psychology paper today. I haven't even started.	
B: It's due today? Are you gonna manage okay?	
A: I hope so. Do you know anything about children and TV violence?	
B: I know a little about children and TV violence. But I don't know enough to help you write a paper.	
A: Oh well. I guess I'm on my own.	

Task 12

Now look at this excerpt from a lecture where the instructor is explaining what the upcoming quiz will be like. Identify the instances of ellipsis. With a partner, try to use the full forms of the sentences.

1. **Student 1:** We having a quiz today?

2. **Instructor:** Yeah. Actually. *<laugh>* Wouldn't want you to get out of shape. *<laugh>* Real short one, though. Multiple choice. Real easy.

3. **Student 2:** The last one was multiple choice too, but it was, twelve, multiple choices. This a real multiple choice?

4. **Instructor:** Well this is only three. You got a better shot at this one.

5. **Student 3:** Is it based on the reading or the notes?

6. **Instructor:** The reading. You do the reading?

7. **Student 3:** Didn't have time.

8. **Instructor:** *<laugh>* It's comparatively easy . . . and remember it doesn't count against you. Just a chance to, make some points.

9. **Student 4:** Counts against you if everybody else does well.

10. **Instructor:** Yeah, well. Maybe. You plan on not doing well? Anyone else?

(Based on MICASE. Intro Oceanography Lecture, File ID: LEL305JU092)

We offer one final comment on ellipsis. The examples shown are rather informal exchanges. Indeed the less formal the speech, the more likely sentences will be ellipted. When a speaking event is more formal, as in a meeting with a person of authority or perhaps a more formal presentation, it may not be so appropriate to delete grammatical elements. So, unless you are on friendly terms with the head of your department, it may not be okay to say, "Got a sec?"

DVD Task
Unit 5: Telling Stories
Scenes 1–2

In each of these scenes, a student is recalling a memorable event. The first story is about a lesson learned about cheating; the second story is about meeting a famous person.

Working in groups of three or four, tell a story about one of these topics:

- a well-known or important person that you met
- a lesson learned when you were younger
- someone in your family or community who has had a strong influence on you
- a celebration that you fondly remember (for instance, a birthday, holiday, family reunion, or wedding)

Be sure to give details. Listeners can ask questions to encourage their partners to elaborate.

Personal Narratives in University Classes

Although we often think that classroom discourse centers on the transmission of disciplinary knowledge, there is, in fact, a lot of other kind of talk going on between students and instructors. There may be joking around, general talk about sports or the weather at the beginning of class, or perhaps discussion of current events. In addition to this kind of talk, you may be surprised that it is not uncommon for U.S. instructors to also tell personal stories or narratives. Personal narratives can be found in lectures of all disciplines from engineering to the social sciences (Dyer and Keller-Cohen 2000).

Why do instructors tell stories? Whether they occur in an academic or a non-academic setting, narratives allow instructors to reveal a little bit of who they are and to create an identity. Narratives can also help explain or make a point. When instructors tell a personal story, they are straddling two worlds: one in which they are seen as a content expert and another in which they are just a regular person with families, mortgages, and non-academic interests such as sports.

Task 13

Read this rather long excerpt from a class discussion about a book that was made into a movie. Answer the questions.

1. **Instructor:** I must say, I saw the movie first. Then I read the book, in English. Then I read the book in Spanish. Then I saw the movie again. And, my own view is that a lot of what I saw in the movie, seemed a little disjointed. And only when I saw, when I saw in the book how those must've actually been flashbacks or just, you know expanding episodes, did I realize why it was put in there. So I found the movie much better on second viewing after having read the novel. So, personally, I found the movie less, well integrated. You guys know that the director of the movie is the husband of the woman who wrote the book. Arau is Esquivel's husband so, it's a a power couple in Mexico. Uh, I saw some nods so, some of you also had my view that the book, the movie was was harder than the book. The movie was good, right? You know that movie made more money than any other foreign language movie in America up until that time. Liz?

2. **Student 2:** I haven't seen the movie, but I just noticed that, the people who spoke—and your view is the same—that whatever they saw or read first was harder to follow. She said she saw the movie first and that was, harder. [**Instructor:** Interesting] so . . . .

3. **Instructor:** Is that right? Is there anybody for whom that is not true? Is there anybody for whom that is, it's not true for you. Speak, please.

4. **Student 3:** Well, it's because I read the first couple pages of the book, *<laugh>* and then I read the movie . . . I watched the movie, then I read the book again. So I wasn't lost at all ever. *<laugh>*

5. **Instructor:** Ahh, so the book made a nice guide to the movie. Right. Okay, alright. it is confusing though which I must say, I find really kind of amazing, when you realize the exquisite simplicity of the language. I mean they're not complicated sentences. There aren't very odd adjectives. And it's it it's not like Faulkner at all you know. It's just you you can read every sentence clearly, and yet there's something wild about it. Um, do you guys like the book? [**Students:** Yes] Okay good. Good me too. I read it again this morning and, between eleven and four, but anyway *<laugh>* uh, and I must say I liked it better again. Uh, so maybe this is one of those ones that that you keep coming back to. I also feel kind of a, a special relationship to this book because of my grandma Mahler, um, my father's mother. I remember this quite vividly. When I was a little boy, um and I mean little like, three, my folks would park me at my grandmother's house sometimes. Years later I found out it was because their marriage was precarious and they probably, needed to get rid of me, um so they could work out other things. But what did I know, right? I mean I was going to grandma's house. And grandma, who was born in Russia, would make me often, potatoes and cream, which, for, Eastern Europeans that means sour cream and either baked or boiled potatoes. She made these so-called new potatoes you know with the thin skin. She would boil 'em. And grandma would set out this enormous

bowl of sour cream, and sit down opposite an enamel table. I can picture it vividly to this day . . . a metal table top, you know covered with some enamel so that you know nothing got through it. I mean you could chip it with a screwdriver, but that was all you could do to it. Um, and grandma would sit opposite me. It was just the two of us. It was folded it up so it was just a two person table, and she'd she'd sit there a- and I'd have the bowl and she would have, in her lap—she'd be wearing an apron—she'd have a washcloth, I mean a . . . what do you call it? Dishwashing, what do you call that yeah?

6. **Students:** Dishtowels

7. **Instructor:** Dishtowel. thank you. Right it was not a washcloth. Dishtowel. Good. How do you say in English? Right? A dishtowel covering her lap and she'd reach under the dishtowel, take out a couple of potatoes, and say *ess Erechel ess* (trans. "eat, little Eric, eat"). So I, you know, *Erechel* would *ess,* and then I would finish the couple of potatoes and there'd still be more sour cream and she'd say so you want another potato? And I'd say sure, and out would come another potato. And I, it was like an endless. . . I never ran out of potatoes. I don't know where grandma got them from. She never had to go back to the stove. It was as if she were giving birth to potatoes, *<laugh>* you know it was like, constant. And every time I have read this book or seen this movie, I'm always reminded of my grandmother, with this endless supply of potatoes. And it reminds me that there's something going on here. It's it goes right back to the fairy tale roots that we talked about the first week of class that, you don't have to say I love you. All you have to do is give somebody food, and that indicates a relationship. And I feel that when I read this. And so, when I see the variations on it . . . well what if you cry into the food while you're making it or what if you feel anger while you're making the food and so on. It sort of resonates for me as if the fairy tale world were becoming a real world. That to me justifies, um, having a book made out of recipes. And this is really weird. I mean, do you guys know of any books like this? I know of a couple that are vaguely like this, but none exactly. Anybody know any books that are even vaguely like this. Yes please?

8. **Student 4:** *A Year in Provence* by Peter Mayle.

9. **Instructor:** Good. You wanna describe it?

(Based on MICASE. Fantasy in Literature Lecture, File ID: LEL300SU076)

1. At what point does the instructor start his personal narrative? Underline the words that signal this.

2. What is the story about?

3. How does he make a connection back to the content of the lecture? Underline where the transition occurs.

4. Can you think of any classes you've had where the instructor or another student has used a personal narrative? If yes, describe the situation and the story as best you can remember.

5. If you were a member of this class, would you want to contribute to the discussion? How? Would you perhaps tell a story?

Task 14

Share a short personal narrative or story about a memorable experience with some members of your class. You could talk about a memorable event in your life or perhaps a family member that you are or were close to. You might find some of these story openers useful.

I remember when I . . .   When I was little, I . . .

When I was younger, I . . .   When I was living in ___, I used to . . .

When I was about ___ years   I remember one time when I was about
old, I . . .   ___ years old, I . . .

Some Final Thoughts about Class Participation

You have seen that there are a variety of ways to participate in class. There is no single correct way to do so; what is important though is to recognize that in many college or university classes, participation is expected, encouraged, and maybe even graded. Thus the strategies you have learned should give you confidence to be an active participant in your classes. Here are some helpful reminders:

- Try to say something in class early in the semester—even a question can help give you confidence to participate.
- Consider using the comments of other students as starting points for your comments.
- If you think the opportunity for commenting has passed, use expressions to move the discussion back. For example,

   I'd like to go back to what you said a minute ago.

   I'd like to go back to what he/she said about . . .

   Could I ask something about what you said before? I was wondering . . .

   Could we go back to what he/she said about . . .

- Try to prepare for each class. If you have done the homework, you will find it easier to make comments. Ask questions. If you are wondering about something, chances are someone else is, too.
- Think about class participation as practice for future situations where you may be expected to talk—a group project, an internship, or a new job.
- Most students and teachers tend to enjoy classes where students participate. Consider your participation as a contribution to a positive classroom atmosphere.
- If you are really worried about talking in class, discuss your concern with your instructors after class or in office hours. Perhaps you and your instructors can find ways for you to be included in class discussion.

DVD Task
Unit 5: Gestures, Facial Expressions, and Body Language
Scene 1

This scene features a discussion about gestures, facial expressions, and body language. Some interesting cultural differences come up in the discussion.

Watch the DVD, and make a list of the gestures, facial expressions, and body language that are described in the scene. List as many as you can. With a partner or partners, discuss how common you think these gestures are, whether your saw or heard anything surprising, and whether there are any other useful gestures or body language that were not included in the discussion.

After class, look for the use of some or all of these in other contexts, and report your findings to the class. You can collect information from television programs, another class, a public lecture, or perhaps observing people talking in a restaurant. Alternatively, be prepared to discuss the similarities and differences between the United States and another country or culture with regard to the use of gestures and body language.

Pronunciation Focus: Pronouns

Introduction

Words in a sentence or phrase may not be pronounced the same as they would be in isolation. How a word is pronounced is affected by whether a word is stressed or not and by the words immediately surrounding it.

Pronouns are often unstressed and, like other words, how they are pronounced is influenced by the words immediately surrounding them. In many instances, the initial sound of the pronoun is dropped.

Would the pronouns be stressed or unstressed in these sentences? In which of these would the pronoun be connected to the preceding word and the initial sound dropped or changed?

1. We can meet at your office.
2. Did you finish your paper?
3. I heard her exam went well.
4. Was she gonna help?
5. He saw them after class.
6. I graded your papers and I'll give them back to you at the end of class.

Data Collection and Analysis

Part 1: Transcription

With one or two partners, listen to Unit 5, Telling Stories, Scenes 1 or 2 on the DVD, and then choose one to two minutes of speech to transcribe. Make sure that at least two turns consist of more than 2–3 words and contain several pronouns. Each of you should transcribe what you hear, listening to the DVD as many times as you need. You can listen together or individually. Once everyone is done transcribing, compare your transcriptions and try to create a complete transcript of the section you chose. Listen to the DVD again if necessary. Indicate any places in the recording where you cannot figure out what is being said and ask your instructor for some assistance.

Part 2: Analysis

With your partners, mark the pronouns on your transcript. Listen to the DVD clip again, and notice how the pronouns are pronounced. Write some observations on how the pronouns are pronounced in context.

Part 3: Report to the class

Your report should provide the following information:

1. Remind your listeners of the focus of your investigation. Which pronouns did you examine?

2. What, if anything, made it difficult to hear the pronouns. Was it the other words surrounding them? The recording? The speakers' rates of speaking? Characteristics of the speakers' pronunciations?

3. What are your group's observations on the pronunciation of pronouns in context? What, if any, other interesting pronunciation observations did your group make?

Part 4: Production

With a partner, read aloud and/or role-play your transcript, paying special attention to sentence stress and pronunciation of the pronouns in context.

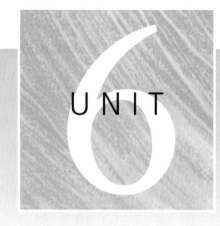

Discussions and Panel Presentations in the Classroom

In this unit, we will focus on student-led discussions and presentations. While they may not be common in every field, discussion and group presentation skills transfer to other contexts, such as seminar classes, journal clubs, and research group meetings, not to mention class participation. Even in larger lecture-type classes, the trend is moving to more interactive ways of teaching. Research shows that active discussion between teachers and students, or even between students, develops critical thinking and deepens understanding of the material (Nicol and Boyle 2003). In addition, working collaboratively on group projects can develop skills that future employers rate highly (Levin 2003). Martin Sanders' (2008) essay in the *Chronicle of Higher Education* describes how he, as an English professor, has tried incorporating more collaborative assignments in his courses because as students enter the workforce they "will be expected to function well in cooperative situations and to understand the dynamics of leadership. Successful work in many professions is based on a symbiotic relationship between good leadership and team work. To function well in a professional setting, you need to be either a good leader or a good collaborator."

Discussions and panel presentations can seem intimidating; however, you will find them more manageable after this unit. We will look at discussions and panel presentations separately, but many of the skills used in discussions will apply to the panel presentation context as well. By the end of the unit you should be able to:

- choose appropriate topics and readings for discussion
- create appropriate questions for discussion
- recognize and use language for giving and getting opinions
- recognize and use language to agree/disagree/hedge
- effectively lead and/or participate in a discussion
- effectively plan and participate in a group (panel) presentation
- introduce topics in a panel
- link speakers in a panel
- use visuals/slides to support a point
- handle question/answer sessions.

Part 1: Discussions in the Classroom

An academic classroom discussion may be set up in different ways. Many students will take classes that expect students to participate in class discussions led by their instructors or teaching assistants. These discussions are typically based on an article or text that everyone has been assigned to read. In some classes, students (individually or in pairs) will be assigned to lead a discussion on a given topic or a reading from the class. As with an instructor-led discussion, everyone in the class may have read the assigned article or text. In other classes, students will be responsible for choosing a reading on which the discussion is based. As you can see, discussions may have unique requirements as part of a particular course. This unit focuses more generally on the organizational strategies and language used in discussions that prepare you for participating in a student-led discussion based on a student-chosen reading on an academic topic. The actual discussion task appears on page 169 (Task 11).

Discussion Structure

Prior to the discussion, the leader will provide a short reading or article that everyone will read. The discussion will then assume this structure.

- The leader will give a brief summary of the reading and provide relevant context or background information.
- The leader will initiate the discussion with a question.
- The leader and participants will proceed with the discussion, exchanging opinions and ideas about the topic.
- The leader will bring the discussion to a close.

Task 1

Discuss these questions with a partner.

1. What do you think is the role of a discussion leader?

2. What do you think is the role of the participants?

3. What challenges are there in fulfilling these roles?

Roles for Discussion Leaders

Discussion leaders will have to do some preparation in advance to ensure that the discussion will flow smoothly. The primary duties of the leader are to have read and become familiar with the readings or materials on the chosen topic; to have prepared a brief summary/introduction, appropriate questions, and follow-ups; and to have a conclusion/wrap-up statement ready. In addition, the leader needs to keep track of the time and manage the group by encouraging everyone to speak or providing chances for everyone to speak. The leader needs to listen well, maybe taking notes as people are speaking in order to keep track of the evolving discussion.

Roles for Participants

As a participant, you also need to prepare by reading and becoming familiar with the discussion materials and listing questions you have. Often students feel pressure to make an important comment or express a clearly thought-out opinion, while in fact lively discussion comes from participants asking questions, figuring things out as they go, and reacting to other comments and opinions, which cannot necessarily be planned. Participants need to listen well and be ready to interrupt if necessary.

Discussion Topics

One of your first jobs then is to decide on a discussion topic and the accompanying reading material. Lively discussions usually occur when the topic is interesting, relevant, and perhaps controversial (i.e., people have strong opinions for or against). It may be best to avoid topics that will evoke too strong a response like abortion or political topics. For our purposes, topics of general interest for a mixed group of students work best; in other classes, topics will be more specific.

Task 2

Let's look at choosing a topic first. Discuss these questions with a partner.

1. What are some current topics of interest that could be used in a discussion?

2: What are some sources for topic ideas? Where can you find topics of interest?

If you are practicing discussion skills in a class with people from a variety of backgrounds or from different academic disciplines, keep your audience in mind. This information will also help you determine appropriate topics.

Task 3

It is easy to think of broad topic ideas that could be interesting and controversial but that may in fact be so broad that there is no focus to the discussion. Some possible topic suggestions are given. With your partner(s), decide if the topic is too broad, too narrow, too controversial, or OK. For the topics that are too broad or too narrow, come up with a revised topic idea. The first example is done for you.

Topic	Too Broad?	Too Narrow?	Too Controversial?	OK
Ban smoking.	X			
Revision: Ban smoking in all public bars and restaurants.				
Recycling should be mandatory on college campuses.				
Revision:				
Students should not be allowed to record lecture classes.				
Revision:				
Cell phone use while driving should be illegal.				
Revision:				
High school students must do volunteer work as a graduation requirement.				
Revision:				

For homework: Look for some interesting short articles that could be the basis of your discussion. Bring two or three to class. You will use these later to practice summarizing.

Summarizing

For our class discussions, the discussion leader will begin by giving some background information for the discussion and then briefly summarize the content of the article or text that everyone has read in preparation for the discussion. The summary serves the purpose of reminding everyone what the reading is about. If there are students in the group who for some reason did not read the article, it will give them some information that will hopefully allow them to participate in the discussion. When summarizing, you will focus on the main ideas of the article, and typically you will refer to the author of the article.

To illustrate various features of discussions, we are using excerpts from a transcript of a class discussion on the topic of ecological architecture. The class consisted of native and non-native speakers of English who are graduate students in the School of Architecture. The discussion was led by a student, Robert, and lasted about 50 minutes. In this particular discussion, the students had to read several texts, so throughout the discussion both the leader and the participants refer to the readings and give brief summaries of the authors' ideas. Let's look at how they do this.

In the first example, Robert, the discussion leader, refers to an article written by a woman. The student in the second example, Kwanghee, refers to a different article, written by a man. The underlined phrases in these examples show ways the speakers refer to something they have read. These phrases precede summaries, which can be as brief as one sentence, or much longer.

EXCERPT 1

Robert: Yeah, I think maybe <u>it's a good time to talk a bit more about the "Taking Shape" article</u> too, where I think <u>she makes more of the argument that</u> um there has to be a sense of beauty for something to have meaning. I took that from the reading quite a bit and . . . I'm, <u>she argues that</u> we have a biodiversity of ecology but not a biodiversity of buildings, um so maybe bring that to the conversation too. The necessity that maybe architecture's role is to make people aware through beauty of the need to respect systems—ecological, social, cultural, or . . . .

(Based on Academic Speaking and Writing for Architects. Class Discussion)

EXCERPT 2

Kwanghee: <u>My article is about</u> ah tradition and traditional knowledge. <u>The author of this article, uh, maintains that</u> the post modernist's approach to history is not a real approach to history, it's like a pastiche or it's devoid of context and content. So it's not a real historical approach. <u>So the author,</u> uh <u>the title of this article is "Growing respect for traditional knowledge,"</u> so the author, in the author's opinion the real respect for traditional knowledge is like the example of the Egyptian architect Hassan Fathy, who shows genuine historical respect. <u>And he, the author, he gives some examples</u> in the history of imperial countries.

(Based on Academic Speaking and Writing for Architects. Class Discussion)

Task 4

With your partners, read these excerpts (they are not connected). Find examples of the language used to refer to an article, a reading, or an author. Fill in the chart on page 155. One has been done for you as an example. Then go to the MICASE database, and search for some of the same words/phrases. Do you find any of the same ones? Similar ones?

EXCERPT 1

Jaemin: Yeah, this article is about technology and um the author says technology has two faces or characteristics and one is to build something, the other is destroy something. Our environment ah has been long been influenced by the technology so the author mentions that we can change our environmental architecture by using the technology.

(Based on Academic Speaking and Writing for Architects. Class Discussion)

EXCERPT 2

Yi: Ah the article talks about the urban future. He says the increase in recent years of the Internet or telecommunications, ICT technologies, we think we work less, use our cars less if we telecommute, and we can have more leisure time so we can be in a more natural environment outside our offices. But in this article it says actually people work more than before because of the Internet we spend more time in front of the computer. Uh so the article also says it's uh it's true we spend more time than before in office buildings so maybe we should concentrate more on how to design the skyscraper or how to uh make a modern building more humane or environmental . . . .

(Based on Academic Speaking and Writing for Architects. Class Discussion)

EXCERPT 3

Steve: Uh, last week, the *New York Times,* ran an article about mathematics, with the title "Math Emerges Blinking into the Glare of the Pop World." This article describes a new booming market for popular math books. Uh it quotes an editorial claiming that the present time is a golden age for popularization of mathematics. It attributes a surge in interest to mathematics to the British mathe- mathematician Andrew Wiles, who made, mathematics headlines around the world, uh for solving, the most famous problem in the history of mathematics . . . .

(Based on MICASE. Public Math Colloquim, File ID: COL385MU054)

EXCERPT 4

Jonathan: Okay this is one thing I would like to end with which I thought was really interesting there's this article by Michael Silverstein. Um, and let me tell you a little bit of this article, if I can find it here. Okay this article is in um the *Journal of Linguistic Anthropology* and he has an article "Encountering Language and Language of Encounter in North American Ethnohistory," and one of the things he says is that if you're gonna look at a language contact phenomenon in native North America or the Americas when dealing with uh Indian languages . . . .

(Based on MICASE. Bilingualism Student Presentations, File ID: STP355MG011)

EXCERPT 5

Barb: . . . alright in uh, Dr Duderstadt's, Duder- I can't pronounce [**Sarah:** Duderstadt] Duderstadt [**Sarah:** Yup] uh article he focused on a change from, um, the need to change, uh the social construct between the university and the community in general. . . . There're, I think five themes that he concentrated on that would be like significant in the future discussion of higher education and the three of them I discussed were diversity, uh interactive and collaborative methodology or pedagog- pedagogy, and then uh, becoming more a learning center. In regards to diversity, he made a good argument for diversity and why it's important to the university . . . .

(Based on MICASE. Politics of Higher Education Seminar, File ID: SEM495SU111)

EXCERPT 6

Pamela: . . . because um in the article that we read um it says that even very proficient second language learners still have problems with pragmatic concepts so we would like to see how they are really different.

(Based on MICASE. Second Language Acquisition Student Presentations, File ID: STP355SU011)

Language Used to Refer to an Article or Reading		Language Used to Refer to an Author	
In the Excerpts	Also in MICASE?	In the Excerpts	Also in MICASE?
My article is about		She argues	
		He gives some examples	

Task 5

List all the verbs used to refer to an article or an author in Excerpts 1 and 2 on page 153 as well as Excerpts 1–6 in Task 4. What tense is used?

Verbs: _____

_____

What other verbs could you use in summarizing? _____

_____

Task 6

Using an article of your own or one provided by your instructor, underline the main points or ideas. Then practice telling a partner or small group about the article, referring to the author or the reading. Try using some of the phrases you listed in the chart on page 155. Take turns summarizing your articles.

Discussion Questions

In Unit 2, we discussed questions in the context of interviewing someone. Some of the same suggestions apply in the discussion context. For example, yes/no questions usually do not generate much discussion, but if a follow-up question is used, it will encourage discussion.

The discussion leader should start with a focused question after giving some background information. Vague or overly broad questions might result in silence. Imagine you want to discuss whether using cell phones while driving should be made illegal. If you start with a question like, *Does anyone have any ideas about this?* or *So, what do you think about it?* you may not get a response. Instead, ask something more specific, like *Do you agree we should ban cell phones while driving?* Since this is a yes/no question, a follow-up *Why or why not?* would then get the discussion going.

Although the leader usually starts things off with a well-framed question, everyone in the discussion can ask questions. All participants can help keep the discussion moving ahead by asking questions. In fact, if you feel unsure about giving your opinion or adding a comment, asking a question is a good way to start participating in a discussion. Sometimes it is a good strategy to ask someone to comment on the topic or issue based on their own experiences. International students bring a unique perspective to their classes and to the academic community. If it is relevant, commenting on something from your own cultural perspective adds to a discussion (e.g., *In Japan we have a new law about cell phone use when driving. It's . . .*).

Task 7 looks at some of the questions that came up during the architecture class discussion. You will notice that the discussion leader, Robert, is not the only person asking questions.

Task 7

Read these excerpts from the architecture class discussion, and answer the questions.

EXCERPT 1

Yi: Actually I'm more curious about ecological architecture, but I'm curious about how much, maybe the author has talked about it but does anyone know how much energy is wasted in buildings? I mean I mean uh how can the authors so emphasize ecological architecture? Do they know that the buildings waste a lot of energy? Do they have this kind of information?

(Based on Academic Speaking and Writing for Architects. Class Discussion)

EXCERPT 2

Kwanghee: Environmentally sound buildings are not usually, I think, in my opinion usually are not appreciated by architecture schools, we just build these amazing buildings. Do you think, do you believe these trends can be changed?

Aidan: Didn't one of the readings talk about that?

(Based on Academic Speaking and Writing for Architects. Class Discussion)

EXCERPT 3

Aidan: Doesn't, wasn't, I thought in this reading "Taking Shape" reading the first couple pages where she talks about Frank Gehry and Peter Eisenman for a little bit, not saying that *they*'re making ecological buildings but she says that their sense of design might be the future of ecological design. Don't you think, I mean we're talking about the cost of materials right now and but we're not developing materials usually but we're deciding how to put them together, so isn't that where, that's where we can make ecology afford-able, through good design? *<pause>* Anybody wanna challenge me on that?

(Based on Academic Speaking and Writing for Architects. Class Discussion)

EXCERPT 4

Aidan: If if if every person in Korea today said they wanted a traditional house would there be enough trees?

Kwanghee: No.

Taechun: But we could choose to use the good features of traditional architecture and get rid of the bad . . . .

(Based on Academic Speaking and Writing for Architects. Class Discussion)

EXCERPT 5

Youngchul: If we choose to live in traditional Korean houses . . . then we don't need to use up energy for heating or cooling. We should live like they did in the past.

Kwanghee: That can't be accepted by modern Korean people.

Aidan: Really? [**Jaemin:** *<laughs>*] [**Aidan:** No air conditioning?] [**Mindy:** No air conditioning]

Robert: Jaemin, what do you think about that?

Jaemin: Uh I think choosing material and structure seems to be depend not only on economic or ecological issues but also the notion of aesthetics, and variation of aesthetics of ordinary people, I mean . . .

(Based on Academic Speaking and Writing for Architects. Class Discussion)

EXCERPT 6

Jaemin: Are there any rules or regulations about ecological building in the U.S.?

Stephen: Right now it's all voluntary isn't it?

Mindy: You get rewards for it, so you have like tax free, depending on what percent of sustainability you have you can get tax breaks.

Stephen: And also there's a lot of government initiatives right now. Is it like that in Korea, do you have initiatives like that?

(Based on Academic Speaking and Writing for Architects. Class Discussion)

1. For each excerpt, underline the questions, and discuss whether the question would be likely to encourage discussion or not.

2. Find examples of yes/no questions. Can you think of follow-up questions for them?

3. In Excerpt 2 and 6, a question is answered with another question. Why do you suppose this is?

4. In Excerpt 3, after a pause and no one offers an answer, the speaker asks if anyone wants to challenge him. Why?

5. In Excerpt 5, the discussion leader, Robert, starts his question by calling on a specific student. Do you think this is a good strategy? Why?

_____

A common question type is one that uses *or* to give choices. It is important to hear that a choice is being given, and the answer should be one of the choices (there can be more than two choices offered). In the next two examples, Youngchul and Kwanghee both do this when answering, and the discussion continues. Notice what happens in the third example. Yi answers the *or* question as if it were a yes/no question. Because this is so unexpected, it prompts laughter and a restatement of the question. The student then goes on to change the topic and continue the discussion.

EXAMPLE 1

Robert: So are you saying that technology is opposed to tradition, versus being a part of the tradition? You're saying they're two opposing things? *<pause>* Are you saying that's your opinion **or** that's the author's opinion?

Youngchul: His attitude is against the technology. The author says [**Robert:** Yeah] we have to overcome the conflict between the two things.

(Based on Academic Speaking and Writing for Architects. Class Discussion)

EXAMPLE 2

Aidan: He's still stuck in that view? **Or** he's saying that's a view to get away from, to change? That there must be change?

Kwanghee: There must be change. That is, I think, he thinks that is a traditional view of technology so we must a overcome that view of technology.

(Based on Academic Speaking and Writing for Architects. Class Discussion)

EXAMPLE 3

Taechun: . . . and so the Modernists' ideas were misunderstood, I think.

Robert: Yi, do you agree with that **or** disagree?

Yi: Uh yeah. *<laughter>*

Robert: Yes you disagree **or** yes you agree? *<laughter>*

Yi: Actually I'm more curious about ecological architecture, but I'm curious about how much, maybe the author has talked about it but . . . .

(Based on Academic Speaking and Writing for Architects. Class Discussion)

Task 8

For homework, find an article you would like to use for the basis of your class discussion. Prepare a brief summary of the main ideas and five questions (with follow-ups if necessary) that you think would stimulate an interesting discussion. Bring the article and questions to class on the date set by your teacher. Then, with a partner in class, give a brief summary of your article, and discuss and evaluate the questions you wrote. Your partner can think of other questions as well.

Turns in Discussions

What does it mean to get the floor? To have the floor? To give someone the floor?

Typically, turn-taking in discussions requires action on the part of the participants. If you want to contribute, you have to actively work at finding an opportunity to talk, or get the floor. Sometimes it is easy to get the floor, as in this example from a seminar on the politics of higher education. Carolyn sees an opportunity when Lisa pauses at the end of her thought. Carolyn then uses specific language to indicate she wants to get the floor.

> **Lisa:** It's more than just a racial and ethnic kind of diversity it's more of, preparing people preparing students for uh positions of leadership once we graduate from the University of Michigan because it's not going to be unusual for us to work for GM or Ford uh I don't know Chrysler Daimler Chrysler or something like that not in Dearborn or Detroit but in uh say, Asia or South America.
>
> **Carolyn:** I think if I could interrupt you for a second [**Lisa:** Uhuh] I think that's a really important point. And you know diversity as a word has kind of become symbolic . . . .
>
> (Based on MICASE. Politics of Higher Education Seminar, File ID: SEM495SU111)

But more often you will not get such an easy in; you will need to use words and body language, for example leaning in toward the table or making eye contact with the speaker, to show you want to speak. <u>You may need to be persistent in order to get a turn.</u> If you always wait until there is a long pause, until someone takes a breath, or until you think someone has completely finished a sentence, you may never get a chance to speak.

In this example you can see how Aidan starts to interrupt by using the first word of his question, *Does,* then uses *mhm,* and then jumps in with his comments before Kwanghee finishes his sentence.

> **Kwanghee:** But can we regulate it? Using a car is pretty economical in this country but if the U.S. government adds more tax on gas it will no longer be economical. If we add more tax on ecologically harmful materials then relatively ecologically sound materials will become cheaper. So that can be solved. But I wonder what if ecologically sound materials have a similar price as un-ecologically sound materials. In that case will architects design using the sound materials or will they still consider the visual impact more important and use whatever materials they need. [**Aidan:** Does] It's my question. I wonder. I'm very suspicious [**Aidan:** Mhm] about . . . .

> **Aidan:** Doesn't, wasn't, I thought in this reading "Taking Shape" reading the first couple pages where she talks about . . . .
>
> (Based on Academic Speaking and Writing for Architects. Class Discussion)

Overlapping speech is generally not considered rude in the context of discussions or conversations. It may be accidental, or it may serve as a way to keep the discussion or conversation going. If you have a chance to observe classmates having a discussion or even just a conversation, notice how much overlap in speech occurs. You may notice that a speaker talks louder with each attempt to get the floor until eventually succeeding or giving up. If you succeed in gaining the floor, be sure you are ready to speak.

In some discussions, the giving and getting of the floor will seem to flow without much effort. But in many cases the leader needs to actively manage the flow to be sure everyone gets a chance to speak and to be sure the discussion stays on topic. These phrases may be helpful. Can you add to them?

To encourage a quiet classmate

Use the person's name (Excerpt 5 on page 158) and directly ask that person a question.

We haven't heard from (name) yet.

_____

If someone is monopolizing

Let's hear what someone else thinks about that. (name), do you agree with (name)?

Let's hear from someone else and then we can come back to that.

We haven't heard from (name).

Okay first (name) then (name).

_____

To stay on topic

Uh I think we're getting a bit off track.

We seem to be getting away from the topic.

We've kinda moved into a different topic so could we come back to the idea of . . . .

_____

You may already have some idea of the language used in discussion to interrupt, give opinions, agree or disagree, clarify, and hedge. Task 9 gives you the chance to explore and confirm your intuitions.

Task 9

With your partner, first fill in Chart A. Write at least two examples of words/phrases you can use to accomplish the functions listed in the chart in an informal class discussion context in the center column.

Then read the three excerpts on pages 164–67 from the architecture class discussion. With a partner, find words or phrases used for interrupting/getting the floor, giving opinions, restating or clarifying, agreeing, disagreeing, and hedging and add them to Chart B on page 163. Compare what you found to your own examples. What did you find? Share your answers with the class.

Later, search for the words/phrases in MICASE and put yes or no in the third column. Share your findings with the class.

A

Examples of Language for	Example from Our Class	Examples in MICASE?
Interrupting		
Agreement		
Disagreement		
Giving an opinion		
Restating or clarifying		
Hedging		

B

Examples of Language for	Example from Architecture Class Discussion	Examples in MICASE?
Interrupting		
Agreement		
Disagreement		
Giving an opinion		
Restating or clarifying		
Hedging		

EXCERPT 1

Aidan: He's still stuck in that view? Or he's saying that's a view to get away from, to change? That there must be change?

Kwanghee: There must be change. That is, I think, he thinks that is a traditional view of technology so we must a overcome that view of technology. *<pause>* I didn't read that part so I'm not sure.

Taechun: I'm not really sure either but I guess it's about having two different views about one thing, about balancing history or tradition and *<continues summarizing>*.

Youngchul: I think uh the author's attitude about that is that as technology develops we can use it to design freely, we can make various buildings but we I think we usually do opposite and damage or [**Robert:** So are you] or disturb tradition and

Robert: So are you saying that technology is opposed to tradition, versus being a part of the tradition? You're saying they're two opposing things? *<pause>* are you saying that's your opinion or that's the author's opinion?

Youngchul: His attitude is against the technology. The author says [**Robert:** Yeah] we have to overcome the conflict between the two things.

(Based on Academic Speaking and Writing for Architects. Class Discussion)

EXCERPT 2

Robert: My understanding is that buildings, that the built environment is responsible for about 50 percent of the energy [**Yi:** 50 percent] yeah 50 percent.

Emma: I think that when they are talking about traditional architecture they're saying there used to be a better way to make buildings, like where they say they make the mud and the glazing it kinda blocked out the sunlight but right now we're like "oh we'll make everything glass and we'll just use lots of air conditioning" and its very wasteful and it used to be more . . . .

Aidan: But, I'm going to play devil's advocate I'm going to argue for just a second that maybe what we don't understand or fail to see sometimes is that people using um earth to build huts were just using whatever was available to them, and today we're using whatever is available to us. Right? So I mean, I don't know, it's tough to, say, understand where our tradition is going to. You know where any new tradition will come from if all we do now is consume or use as much as possible and that's what sort of what tradition was.

Emma: Right so I think they're saying that new, I don't know what they call it, new urbanism, post global world, rather than just being based off of tradition it should be based off of awareness, because we do have information, if not in this paper, we do have lots of statistics about energy, pollution.

Kwanghee: Environmentally sound buildings are not usually, I think, in my opinion usually are not appreciated by architecture schools, we just build these amazing buildings. Do you think, do you believe these trends can be changed?

(Based on Academic Speaking and Writing for Architects. Class Discussion)

EXCERPT 3

Kwanghee: So if the ecological danger like global warming or the ozone hole, if such a thing is not urgent then the way of Eisenman or Frank Gehry can be our choice, but if ecological danger is so urgent Eisenman should be regarded as a dangerous architect. The key is so how do we know that ecological danger is urgent or not? We have no time to wait for . . .

Aidan: Yeah, but I thought what the article was saying was that knowing, understanding that not all buildings have to be square might make it possible to do, to design buildings so to make the most efficient building it needs to be curved like this *<demonstrates curves>* that they're learning how to shape space in different ways to make it more adaptable so I just thought that was, yeah, not talking about *them* necessarily but talking about the role of the design, that it's important for the designer to understand what materials are affordable and how to use them effectively um that was the way to push ahead with sustain, to make the building sustainable.

Robert: Plus their work is maybe um pioneering fabrication methods too which could then be adapted to a more knowledgeable [**Taechun:** What?] fabrication, the way the buildings are constructed allows for a more intelligent way of building that could then be adapted to a, with a more ecological sensibility. Youngchul, were you going to add something?

Youngchul: Yeah, uh uh I think in this article he says when we design we don't consider the environment. But I don't think so. There are many kind of ways to design the building. If we use just reinforced concrete, we cannot recycle it, it's hard to recycle at any rate but these days we usually use the steel structure, but we can design more freely with the steel structure. I think in Korea we make, we build an airport, in Korea Incheon Airport it has a really free shape, various shapes but it was made with steel structure, and we can recycle the steel. I think Frank Gehry these days Frank Gehry maybe makes the steel structure the most, so we can recycle more.

Taechun: Recycling is not the only factor of sustainability. Maintenance costs such as air conditioning is also important factors of sustainability. We should evaluate Frank Gehry's building or the Incheon Airport, we should evaluate maintenance cost of those buildings.

Youngchul: But we can reduce the damage of our environment. We don't need [**Taechun:** Yes] to use the stone or cement or create any longer.

Kwanghee: So I think the point is we should use recyclable materials *and* [**Youngchul:** And and] make maintenance costs lower. Those points both of them are important. Recycling issue is not the only part [**Youngchul:** Yeah].

Taechun: Many people I think every region has their vernacular solution. In Korea in traditional Korean architecture, we have a kind of thinking architecture should be one part of nature actually because we had no reinforced concrete, we gathered the resources from nature, the wood, mud, stone, we totally built a kind of traditional architecture with with part of nature, not a building *on* nature, just one part in the scene of nature . . . .

Kwanghee: It's a good point but we must be aware of a too romantic view of traditional architecture. Uh actually Korean traditional architecture is called *Han ok. Han ok* is very expensive to build, the materials are *so* expensive nowadays in Korea, because the wood in Korea is very expensive, the wood to build the house. And the air conditioning cost in traditional buildings is *so* high. . . .

(Based on Academic Speaking and Writing for Architects. Class Discussion)

When one participant disagrees with something that another participant has said, it helps to focus on disagreeing with the idea or opinion being stated, not with the person. There should not be a sense that you are "attacking" a person because of his or her ideas. One way to make disagreements less aggressive is to use hedging to soften our negative statements, such as *That solution seems a bit unrealistic* instead of *Your solution will never work.* The hedging language used in discussions is similar to the ways you learned to show politeness in email requests in Unit 3. Hedging is also discussed in Unit 5.

Cautious disagreement can be expressed in a number of ways, for instance, *well maybe so, but* . . . . An interesting way to show partial agreement is with the phrase *yeah, but* . . . . Do you think this is very common in academic speech? If you search MICASE for the phrase *yeah but,* you'll see it appears more than 200 times. Other times we are cautious and may hedge when we are not sure of what we think, but still want to contribute something, for example, by saying, *Well, I guess so* or *I sort of/kind of agree with that.*

This excerpt from a public policy seminar has several examples of hedging. Notice in particular how Michelle is very uncertain about her opinion, yet still is confident enough to contribute to the discussion. The phrases in bold highlight hedging.

Josh: Well the other thing is, we've talked about what our main concerns are with the crack market, the violence it causes and, I think the crack market in many cities are certainly concentrated in areas . . . they're mostly in poor neighborhoods . . . they're mostly poor. So I think, you know it's gonna be hard to pinpoint uh where people are getting crack in some cities but, uh I think by targeting the market it's just, it's gonna be . . . .

Michelle: Yeah but I kinda think two things about that, **I think first**, you have to look at the reason why why crack is targeted . . . **there might be** something behind the original motivation behind why you decided to target, **you've kinda gotta examine** that. Second thing, is that **I think that, and you kinda mentioned it** . . **I don't know if I agree that** the only segments of communities affected by the drug war are hard core drug users . . . **and I just I'm not sure that I a hundred percent agree** that it's as targeted . . . .

Josh: Right. Well well, my response to that is how many people've been affected by the systemic violence associated with the crack trade? . . . that's an issue and that's a problem but, I think just as much of an issue are the effects that you know law abiding people in those communities have to face every day. Because of this high systemic violence associated with the crack market.

> **Michelle: Yeah but I mean, I do think, I mean I think** about fifteen minutes ago, we had a long discussion about crime and . . . you know communities are really trying to balance, a lot of these issues.
>
> **Nick:** Laura did you have a follow-up on this point? You had your hand up earlier.
>
> **Laura: I just, I had wanted to say something** about the quote that Justin read which **I think it's a little bit misleading** how it portrays who's arrested for using drugs . . . .
>
> (Basd on MICASE. Graduate Public Policy Seminar, File ID: SEM340JG072)

Giving Opinions and Active Listening

If you were able to search MICASE for the phrases you found in Tasks 9 and 10, you will have noticed that the most common way to give your opinion is to say *I think*. In fact, the phrase appears more than 4,000 times in the MICASE data, while the phrase *in my opinion* appears just 15 times. After *I think*, what other phrases were most common for giving an opinion?

If you state an opinion in a discussion, it usually is something you actually believe, for example, *I think cell phone use while driving is dangerous.* But if everyone seems to agree on a point, and you want to encourage some discussion by bringing up the opposing view, you might do what Aidan does in the following example.

> **Aidan:** But, I'm going to play devil's advocate I'm going to argue for just a second that maybe what we don't understand or fail to see sometimes is that people using um earth to build huts were just using whatever was available to them, and today we're using whatever is available to us.

Notice how he says, *I'm going to play devil's advocate.* By announcing this, he shows he is going to argue a position that he personally doesn't believe, but he wants to bring up for the sake of the argument. This strategy is used to encourage others to think of alternative perspectives, challenge existing opinions, and stimulate more discussion. It is a safe way to argue for or against something even if it is not your own personal opinion. Another way to do this is to simply use *what if.* In this MICASE example of a class discussion on the ethics of printing a photo of a murder victim in the newspaper, notice how the instructor tries to encourage more discussion by getting the students to argue views they may not believe. Notice the language in bold used to do this.

Dante: Was it the reporter or the photographer? Which one was it? Who said it was okay?

Instructor: Yeah I don't know whether the family was the first to say it was okay.

Jim: They weren't.

Dante: Right.

Instructor: But, uh now you know what I'm gonna ask you next right? **What if** the family had said no? **[Several students:** Mhm]

Dante: No way.

Instructor: The family says no, and you say okay we don't run the picture.

Dante: Exactly.

Instructor: Just for the sake of argument somebody disagree. You don't have to personally agree with it, just advocate the position. Yeah?

Andy: You're an independent newspaper and you've decided already that you wanna run the photo because it's gonna affect people and it's gonna make people understand the context of the murder more, and so it's gonna be serving the public good by showing this photograph and so you should show it anyway.

(Based on MICASE. Ethics Issues in Journalism Lecture, File ID: LES220SU140)

When reading (or even listening to) transcripts of discussions, you miss the visual picture of what the participants are doing during the discussion. Can you think of ways to show you are an active participant, even if you are not speaking?

Being an active listener is an important way to show you are participating. You can use body language to show you are listening. Non-verbal cues, like nodding in agreement or shaking your head in disagreement, also indicate you are active in the discussion. Leaning in toward the table (if you are seated around a table for example) or shifting your position so you can see the speaker also shows you are engaged. When speaking, it's good to keep eye contact with as many of those in the group as you can; you don't usually want to talk to just one person. Using backchannel cues, like *mhm, okay, uhuh,* or *yeah* shows you are paying attention. Remember how these words can be used when you want to interrupt, too. Active listening skills are also very useful in office hours, other classroom situations, and conversation.

Task 10

This activity gives you a chance to consolidate some of the language you have learned by practicing giving your opinion on the following topics.

Work in pairs on this task, exchanging opinions and agreeing or disagreeing about the topic. One of you may want to play the devil's advocate. Practice active listening techniques as well. Report what your group discussed by briefly summarizing and restating your ideas for the whole class. Then, repeat the task with a new partner and a new topic.

Topic 1: Should school uniforms be required for students in elementary school/middle school/high school?

Topic 2: Should students be allowed to use laptops during lecture classes?

Topic 3: Should international students be required to take English language classes after they are admitted to a university?

Topic 4: Topic of your own choice.

Task 11

Prepare for class discussions. You may be a discussion leader and/or a participant. Your instructor will provide details on the discussion groups and schedules. Refer to the Discussion Reminders to help you prepare.

DISCUSSION REMINDERS

For the Leader

- Choose an appropriate topic and reading/article for discussion.
- Prepare a summary of the article/topic, giving relevant background information or context.
- Prepare questions and follow-ups to encourage discussion.
- Show you are actively listening.
- Keep track of time.
- Get everyone involved.
- Conclude.

For Participants

- Prepare by reading the article and thinking about the topic for discussion.
- Have questions ready.
- Interrupt as needed.
- Participate by asking questions and by adding comments or your opinion on the topic.
- Show you are actively listening.

Discussion Feedback

After you finish your discussion, it is a good idea to reflect on how it went—what things went well, and what things could be improved. With the group, discuss the strengths and weaknesses of the discussion.

Part 2: Panel Presentations in the Classroom

Panel presentations, like classroom discussions, provide an opportunity for you to interact and practice skills that may be useful in a future workplace. In addition to the obvious benefit of gaining practice and confidence speaking in public, panel presentations provide practice in negotiating, listening, and organizing. Working as a team also gives you a chance to learn valuable interpersonal skills.

You can look for opportunities to see panel presentations on your own campus by searching your school's calendar of events. These presentations are usually open to all students or even the general public. For example, a panel on *Study Abroad Options for Students* might be organized to attract new applicants to the school's study abroad program, or a panel on *Alcohol Use and Abuse on Campus* might be offered to increase awareness of drinking habits of students. This panel could include presenters from a variety of backgrounds, such as the dean of academic affairs, and representatives from the student health service, the campus public safety office, and the campus housing office. You can also attend panel presentations on field-specific topics at regional or national conferences.

The focus here is on panel presentations as part of a class. In this type of presentation, a small group of students is responsible for presenting information on a topic to their classmates. The topic may be assigned by the instructor or chosen by the group. Group members usually divide their topic into several subtopics so that each group member has a specific area to investigate and present. Panel presentations may focus on presenting factual information or may focus on presenting different opinions about controversial topics. Visuals are commonly a part of the presentation and could include maps, charts, graphs, or pictures that are presented on overheads or on slides. Typically, the panel ends with a question and answer session.

Let's look in more detail at the planning steps and what the presenters need to do.

Panel Presenter Roles

Knowing the role of each member of the panel will help make for a well-organized panel presentation. Typically a panel or group presentation will consist of three or four students with these roles:

The first presenter (the facilitator) is usually responsible for

- introducing the topic and possibly the other speakers
- giving an overview of the presentation
- presenting one subtopic
- keeping track of time for all presenters
- making concluding remarks
- facilitating the question and answer period at the end.

All presenters, including the facilitator, are responsible for

- introducing themselves (if needed) and their subtopics
- clearly presenting one subtopic within the assigned time limit
- using visuals as needed
- making a smooth transition from the speaker before them to the speaker after them.

Panel Presentation Topics and Organization

Successful panel presentations deal with topics that are interesting, current, and relevant to the audience. The topic of your panel presentation may be assigned by your instructor, or your group may have to choose one. Regardless of whether you need to choose a topic or are assigned one, you will need to keep in mind the time limit for the entire presentation and make sure the scope of the topic is appropriate for the time allowed. Time should be balanced among all of the presenters. This could range between five and ten minutes per person or about 20 to 30 minutes total for the panel, depending on what your instructor expects.

Task 12

With your partner, think about how you might approach the topic of Alcohol Abuse on Campus. Complete the chart with possible subtopics, assuming you have four people in the panel group. Some examples have been given.

Presenter	Subtopics/Presenter Roles
1	introduce topic—Alcohol Abuse on Campus define terms used in the presentation give some background information and statistics for our campus
2	
3	
4	
1	conclusion, summarizing question/answer session

An example follows of how students giving a panel presentation on this topic divided up their roles and the subtopics they chose. How does this compare to yours?

Presenter	Subtopics/Presenter Roles
1	• introduce topic, Alcohol Abuse on Campus • overview of the rest of the presentation (who will do what) • discussion of the current situation—including campus statistics, definition of terms, and legal considerations • transition to next speaker
2	• discuss problems of alcohol poisoning and other health risks, drunk driving, and poor academic performance • give examples • transition to next speaker
3	• discuss solutions including alcohol awareness programs on campus, designated driver programs • give examples • transition to next speaker
4	• discuss action students can take to become educated about risks and to learn how to speak up and help someone • give examples • transition back to facilitator
1	• conclude or summarize • initiate question/answer period • facilitate question/answer period • indicate end of presentation

When determining an organizational plan for your topic, consider audience and purpose. The purpose of some panel presentations is to present information and facts while in other presentations the purpose is to persuade the audience to accept a certain perspective. Notice how this group set up their presentation in a problem/solution format—that is, Presenter 1 introduces alchohol abuse as a campus problem; Presenter 2 elaborates on the problems it causes; Presenters 3 and 4 introduce possible solutions or ways to help the situation on campus; and Presenter 1, in concluding, comments on the solutions offered. This format typically includes a situation or context, the problem(s), the solution(s), and some evaluation of the solution(s).

Some common organizational plans that you may already be familiar with include:

- chronological order
- compare and contrast
- advantages/disadvantages or pros/cons
- cause and effect
- classification

Task 13

Work with a partner to suggest a possible organizational scheme for the topics listed. Be ready to explain why you chose the scheme you did.

Topic	Possible Organizational Scheme
Global warming	
Approaches to health care in the U.S. and Indonesia	
The impact of the iPod	
Energy efficient buildings	
Drunk driving	
School uniform policies	

You may have realized that in order to pick a topic and plan the subtopics, you may need to do some research. In the preliminary planning stage, each presenter can do some general research on the topic, checking the Internet or current journals or books (keeping the audience in mind, of course), and then bring their ideas back to the group. The group then meets to negotiate what to include and decide who will do what. We will look at negotiating language later, but now let's focus more on topic choices.

Task 14

Let's assume you're thinking about one of these topics for a panel presentation:

natural disasters	severe weather
wedding traditions	protecting endangered species
genetically modified foods	preserving historic buildings

With your partner/small group, pick one topic, and answer the questions. Use the chart for your notes. Be ready to present your ideas to the class.

1. Evaluate the topic. Is it interesting? Relevant? Current?

    If it is too broad how would you narrow it?

    If it is too narrow how would you broaden it?

2. What subtopics would make sense? How would you assign roles for the topic if you had four presenters on the panel?

3. Decide what organizational strategy you could use, and what order the subtopics should be in so that the presentation flows smoothly.

1. Topic and Evaluation:	
2. Presenter Roles and Subtopics:	
Presenter #1	
Presenter #2	
Presenter #3	
Presenter #4	
Presenter #1	
3. Organizational Strategy:	

Negotiating Panel Preparation—Topics and Roles

When you are assigned to be part of a panel presentation, the group's composition is often determined by the instructor, but what happens next is up to the group. Thus it is useful to become familiar with some of the language used in negotiating the preparation stages of the panel.

Task 15

Read this excerpt of students negotiating a panel topic and deciding on roles. The excerpt is divided into two parts, with some questions after each part.

1. **Miriam:** So, we have to talk about some current health related issue for students, and um I was thinking what about stress, you know, everyone experiences stress and,

2. **Eric:** Hmm, yeah, maybe, but isn't that kinda a big topic, I mean, I don't know, it's pretty broad. Um, how about underage drinking on campus? That's really common.

3. **Tom:** Yeah, I like that but uh is it enough for 30 minutes?

4. **Eric:** Hmm. Then how about alcohol abuse on campus? That could include underage drinking, cuz alcohol abuse is a problem even if you're legal, so it might be more, better to talk about, and we can still talk about underage drinking.

5. **Miriam:** Yeah and um, maybe we can talk about any connections between stress and drinking.

6. **Maria:** Mkay with me, I don't really care either way.

7. **Miriam:** So, everyone okay with it? [**Eric:** Yeah] we'll do alcohol abuse on campus?

8. **Tom:** Mhm [**Maria:** Okay with me] I can live with it.

1. Underline any phrases you think the students use to suggest a topic.

2. Circle any words or phrases the students use to indicate agreement or disagreement.

3. Do you think Miriam is okay that her first topic suggestion was not taken? How do you know (what language does she use to indicate how she feels)?

4. What does Tom mean in Turn 8 when he says, *I can live with it?*

Interaction continues with negotiating roles.

9. **Eric:** Who wants to go, who wants to start? I don't wanna go first.

10. **Tom:** I do. I wanna go first.

11. **Maria:** You do? [**Tom:** Yeah] Really?

12. **Eric:** Okay, I'm okay going second. And I can do something about drunk driving. I know someone who was arrested for that and I could give that as an example. I mean it was really awful what happened, but at least no one got hurt but it made a big impression on my friend and on all of us, really. So I'd like to do that.

13. **Miriam:** Sounds fine with me.

14. **Maria:** Uh, Miriam do you wanna go third, or last? Does it matter to you?

15. **Miriam:** I dunno, could I go third? I just don't want to be last.

16. **Maria:** Whatever you want.

17. **Eric:** Okay, so it'll be like this, me, then Tom, then Miriam, then Maria. Okay?

18. **Maria, Miriam:** Mhm <nodding>

19. **Tom:** Yep. And before we meet next class let's all get more information you know, besides Eric doing drunk driving . . . .

20. **Miriam:** And I still wanna do something about stress. If no one minds.

21. **Tom:** Okay then let's all bring stuff to our next class and then we can decide what exactly to include. Okay?

22. **Eric:** Uhuh. When exactly is the presentation? Did he say? Like do we have a couple weeks to get ready or not that much time?

5. Underline any words or phrases that indicate the students' preferences for the order they will present in or preference of topic.

6. Circle any words or phrases that indicate what a student does NOT want to do.

7. How would you characterize the negotiations? Did everyone end up with what they wanted?

8. Who seems to be in charge? How can you tell?

9. What could you do or say if someone in the group does not agree with any suggestions? What if after Miriam says, *I still wanna do something about stress, if no one minds,* one of the other students says, *You know, I just don't think that fits; there are other better things to include*? If you were Miriam, how could you respond to that?

Useful Phrases for Negotiating

Can you think of any other phrases? How does intonation affect these phrases?

To Make Suggestions	To Show Preference or Agreement	To Show Disagreement
How about . . . ?	I'd like to do	I don't want to do
Do you wanna do . . . ?	I want to	Not really
What if I do . . . ?	Okay	I don't think so
Why don't you . . . ?	Sure. No problem	(silence/no response)
	(silence/no response)	

To Show Concession	To Show No Preference	To Indicate Next Steps
I will if no one else will.	It doesn't matter to me	Let's all bring stuff to our next class.
	Either is fine with me	
	Whatever you want	

DVD Task

Unit 6: Groups
Scenes 1–3

In these scenes, students are negotiating schedules and projects. In Scene 1, the students are trying to arrange a time to work together. Scenes 2 and 3 are two different outcomes of negotiations about what role each group member will have in the upcoming group project.

Watch the pair of negotiating interactions, Scenes 2 and 3. Compare the outcomes of the negotiations. What do you think accounts for the different outcome in Scene 3? Have you ever been in a similar situation to Sun in Scene 2 or Scene 3? What language can you use to strongly voice your preference for what you want to do in a group project?

Starting the Panel Presentation

Let's look at how speakers start their presentations and the strategies they use.

Task 16

These excerpts are introductions given by the first speaker in four different student group presentations. In the first two examples, the students present viewpoints on the war on drugs in the United States. In the second two examples, the students discuss Fetal Alcohol Syndrome and Stress, respectively, in terms of biochemistry. Read the introductions, and then discuss the questions that follow.

INTRODUCTION 1

David: Okay um I'm gonna start us off. I'm gonna basically provide a kinda introduction uh to our arguments, um then I'll turn it over to the two of them. I'd like to start out with some statistics, actually just to get us thinking about some of the issues involved in the war on drugs. . . .

(Based on MICASE. Graduate Public Policy Seminar, File ID: SEM340JG072)

INTRODUCTION 2

Lucy: Okay I'm gonna start um I'm gonna start just by giving a little overview of the justification of the drug war, explain why it's necessary, then Bob will be talking about how crack and cocaine in particular causes crime, or contributes to crime, and then John will go into a little more about the sentencing um of crack versus cocaine. So, as we all know just from watching the news, drugs are a very serious problem in the U.S. . . .

(Based on MICASE. Graduate Public Policy Seminar, File ID: SEM340JG072)

INTRODUCTION 3

Aaron: Alright, um our topic is Fetal Alcohol Syndrome. Today we're gonna look at what it is, how somebody gets it, biochemically we're gonna look at the effects of alcohol on the developing fetus, the symptoms, uh the prevention and then you're gonna get, a brief summary at the end. Uh basically, Fetal Alcohol Syndrome is . . . .

(Based on MICASE. Teaching Biochemistry Student Presentations, File ID: STP175SU141)

INTRODUCTION 4

Lisa: Hi I'm Lisa Webster. We're gonna be talking about stress and cortisol today, and um all the negative effects of that. This is a little, uh it's just a brief outline of what we're talking about first we'll go into a little bit about stress, uh and the different types of it the symptoms, then we'll talk more about cortisol and then we'll debate the two. Um okay, stress is just basically defined as . . . .

(Based on MICASE. Teaching Biochemistry Student Presentations, File ID: STP175SU141)

1. What role does the first speaker in a panel or group have?

2. Look more closely at David's introduction.
   a. What is the group's topic?
   b. What does David mean by *our arguments?*
   c. When he says, *I'll turn it over to the two of them,* who is he talking about?
   d. What are *they* going to do?

3. Look more closely at Lucy's introduction.
   a. How is the word *Okay* used?
   b. What does the phrase *John will go into* mean?
   c. How does she indicate a transition from the overview to starting her part?

4. Which introduction is stronger, David's or Lucy's? Why?

5. Notice the use of *we* vs. *I* in all four introductions. What effect does this have on the audience?

6. In all four introductions, underline examples of the language used to indicate organization.

7. What benefit does giving an overview or "roadmap" in the introduction have on the audience? For the presenters?

_____

It is important to remember that a good overview will clearly introduce the topic, the names of the other panel participants, and the subtopics they will cover. Lucy's introduction is a good example of how this can be done.

Notice how frequently the speakers use the word *gonna* in their introductions. Find examples of the word *gonna* in the excerpts, and underline them. How is this word used?

In addition to providing an overview, a successful introduction to a panel needs to capture the audience's attention as well. The excerpts are not particularly interesting since they start by just announcing the topic. Alternatively, Lisa could have started out like this:

> **Lisa:** Ok, everyone, imagine that right now, instead of a panel presentation, we are going to have an unannounced test on chapter 3 of the text, and it will count for 25 percent of your final grade. Are you feeling some stress? I know I would be really stressed out, in fact I might even have some physical reactions to that news—like my heart would beat faster, my palms might get sweaty, my stomach might feel a bit weird, and even my breathing would get faster. Well all of those are physical reactions to stress. So today we're gonna be talking about stress and . . . [continues with overview].

Would this introduction have gotten your attention? Why would you be more interested in listening to what was going to follow? You can use examples, anecdotes, statistics, a visual image, or a personal story to get people's attention. Consider tapping into what your audience likely knows, as Lisa does here. She knows her audience consists of fellow classmates, all of whom understand the stress of having an unannounced test.

Task 17

Re-write David's introduction on page 179, using an attention-getting opening, as well as a better organizational strategy. Practice reading it out loud to your partner(s).

As Lisa did, try to create a more interesting opening to precede the overviews for Introductions 2 (page 179) and 3 (page 180).

Referring to Other Speakers

As previously discussed, each speaker on a panel has an individual presentation to make, but there must be an overall sense of connection and continuity for the presentation to be successful. Good speakers are aware of and plan for smooth transitions from one presenter to the next. In addition, speakers will show that there is continuity in the presentation by referring to ideas or information covered by another speaker, before or after them.

Task 18

Look at how David's panel from the public policy class makes transitions and refers to other speakers. The excerpts are from the beginning, middle, and/or end of each speaker's turn. Gaps in the turns are indicated by . . . . After reading the excerpts, discuss the questions with your partner(s).

> **David:** Okay um I'm gonna start us off. I'm gonna basically provide a kinda introduction uh to our arguments, um then I'll turn it over to the two of them. I'd like to start out with some statistics, actually just to get us thinking about some of the issues involved in the war on drugs. . . .
>
> *[end]* . . . so, that's the second theme, and so I'll turn it over to Ann now.
>
> **Ann:** Okay um the first question that I would like to ask is whether the successes of the drug war are balanced with . . . .
>
> *[middle]* . . . um, the other costs, David already touched upon some of them um including the harsher penalties and . . . .
>
> *[end]* . . . I think that that is something which is really does raise I think a very valid moral questions and something that we need to consider. Um and I'll turn it over to Mary.
>
> **Mary:** Okay, I'm going to talk about the uh sort of what David talked about in the intro the two pronged approach that we think should be taken to reforming the war on drugs.
>
> *[middle]* . . . uh, first is fifty-fifty, even treatment, like David said our current spending is . . . and I guess that the three of us think that this loss of money could be acceptable if results were being produced, but they're not. As Ann and David talked about we have exploding prison populations which are costly in and of themselves, huge racial disparities. . . . Second thing that we want to talk about is reform of sentencing laws, uh, like David touched on in the early seventies, . . . I think a lot of the things that John discussed are things which are reasonable if there's more crime being associated with the trade if someone gets killed during the trade uh of a of a drug. . . . and the reason why we think why think is because and John did quote a little bit from the Sentencing Commission um Study well I just wanna finish their thought, that there aren't a lot of studies which prove . . . .
>
> *[end]* . . . we should look at the severity of the crime and look at other factors involved when you determine sentencing. And that's it.

(Based on MICASE. Graduate Public Policy Seminar, File ID: SEM340JG072)

1. What does David say to indicate that it is the next speaker's turn? What does Ann say?

2. Here are a few more ways to make a smooth transition to the next speaker. Can you add some of your own?

   I'll hand it over to (name)

   Now (name) will talk about . . .

   _____

   _____

3. Underline the words or phrases used to refer to a previous speaker. List the verbs used. An example has been provided.

   talked about

4. Do you think that referring to a previous speaker is a good strategy? Why?

5. Mary uses extensive references to previous speakers in her part of the presentation. Why do you think this is?

6. There are more examples in MICASE from other presentations of how speakers refer to other speakers or ideas. Here are a few more phrases to add to your repertoire:

   . . . as Yoko pointed out . . .

   . . . just to go along with what Gabriela suggested . . .

   . . . and basically what Martin was saying was . . .

   Can you think of any others?

   _____

It is interesting to contrast the transitions between speakers in the classroom panel example and this example from a somewhat more formal panel presentation given as part of a university sponsored Women in Science conference. Here, there is a moderator whose job it is to introduce the panel members and make transitions between speakers.

Cinda: . . . and I think I'll end now and let my colleagues share their experiences.

Jean (moderator): Okay, thank you Cinda. Um, Joyce Yen is going to speak next, um she is currently a graduate student in the Industrial and Operations Engineering Department, she received her undergraduate degree in mathematics, and she's currently director of the graduate uh chapter of the Society of Women Engineers.

Joyce: Thanks Jean . . . um, as Jean said um I am in Industrial and Operations Engineering and I do come from a math background . . . .

(Based on MICASE. Women in Science Conference Panel, File ID: COL999MX040)

Notice how each speaker thanks the previous speaker. This strategy can be used in classroom presentations, but it is far more common in more formal presentations outside of the classroom, for example at campuswide events or professional conferences.

Referring to other speakers and showing how their ideas connect to yours will show your audience that you have prepared well as a group and have thought about the panel presentation as a whole, as well as the individual parts. It also shows you are listening to each other. It may happen that someone who speaks before you actually gives some of the same information you planned to give (of course, good preparation and practice beforehand would probably keep that from happening). If that is the case, you need to be sure you don't just repeat exactly what was said before. Be flexible in such cases and consider how you will handle it. If you do need to repeat, then referring to the prior speaker is important.

Task 19

Consider these scenarios, and discuss with your partner or small group how you could handle these situations. Share your ideas with the class.

Scenario 1

As you are listening to the presenter before you, you hear him covering some of what you are planning to say. What can you do when it is your turn?

Scenario 2

The presenter before you was supposed to talk about some specific examples that would lead into your part of the presentation. You practiced your part knowing it would follow these specific examples. But she didn't include the examples. What can you do when it is your turn?

Summarizing at the End of the Panel

You may remember the first speaker or facilitator should make some concluding remarks or summarize what the panel has presented, before starting the question/answer session. While these remarks can be prepared in advance, it is necessary for the facilitator to listen carefully to the presentation as it is happening and make adjustments to any prepared conclusion as needed. For example, it's possible one of the presenters will leave out a section of their talk because of time constraints or because they simply forgot it. As a result, you would not want to refer to it in the concluding remarks if it had been omitted.

Task 20

The MICASE database shows these phrases that signal concluding or wrapping up. Place a check (✔) next to the phrases you might use.

_____ So, in conclusion . . .

_____ Well, I guess, in conclusion . . .

_____ In conclusion . . .

_____ I want to conclude . . .

_____ To conclude . . .

_____ I'm gonna try to wrap up.

_____ I'm gonna wrap up.

_____ Just to wrap up . . .

_____ I think we should begin to wrap up.

_____ I wanna wrap up.

These phrases also work in this context although they are somewhat more formal.

_____ As we've heard today . . .

_____ We've covered . . .

_____ Let me conclude by . . .

Can you think of any others?

_____

_____

Question-and-Answer Sessions

Typically a panel or group presentation will end with a question and answer session (Q&A). The first speaker, or facilitator, is usually in charge of starting the Q&A, watching the time, and noting and calling on people in the audience if there are several people who want to ask questions at the same time. Finally, the facilitator will close the presentation, usually by indicating time is up and saying *thank you.*

From student presentation examples in MICASE, we can see that the most common way of asking for questions is this very simple form:

> Any questions?

Other examples in MICASE include the following:

> Do you have any questions?
>
> Does anybody have any questions?
>
> Are there any questions?
>
> So do you guys have any questions?
>
> Alright, any questions?
>
> Does anyone have any questions?
>
> I will entertain questions.
>
> I think we have ten minutes for questions.
>
> Any more questions?

Which of these seem most formal? Most informal? Why? Can you guess in what type of presentation these were used?

Ideally, we should be able to handle most questions—we can hear the speaker just fine; we understand the intent of their question; we know the answer; and we give a complete answer. However, it's not always that easy. You may need to ask for clarification or repetition before answering a question. It's also possible you can't answer a question. The next task gives you a chance to think about how to handle some of these situations.

Task 21

With your partner or small group, list at least two possible ways to respond to these situations.

1. Someone interrupts you during the presentation with a question, but it is something you (or your group member) will talk about next—you need to defer answering.

2. You didn't understand the question—you need to ask for clarification.

3. You didn't hear the question—the speaker's voice was too quiet.

4. You don't know the answer to the question being asked.

5. You have answered a question and want to confirm that you have answered it sufficiently.

6. There is no more time for questions—you need to conclude the session.

You will not likely encounter all of these situations in one presentation, but knowing how to respond if they arise will help you feel ready to handle the Q&A. In this transcript of the Q&A after a student presentation on pharmacogenomics, a technology that uses an individual's genetic information to inform choices in medications, the presenter demonstrates several of these question-handling strategies. Although this is an individual presentation, the speaker's strategies are useful for any Q&A, including panel presentations.

Task 22

Read the transcript and answer the questions with your partner. The presenter is Jiani; Yuji, Tati, and Sojung are different audience members asking questions.

1. **Jiani:** So, that's pharmacogenomics, the new technology, uh I think the potential for this kind of technology is very high and I believe in the future everybody will have personal medicine. Uh okay so does anyone have any questions? Yes? *<looking at Yuji>*

2. **Yuji:** Can you explain to me what does it mean to use genetic information, uh [**Jiani:** Mhmm] I can I can understand a little bit but . . . .

3. **Jiani:** Yeah, uh actually this is because this is a very very new technology, just about 20 years old now so um in the early stage we were just doing research about the drug transporter, or the drug enzyme. The drug transporter is to transport the drug in your body. You take a oral tablet that takes it to your stomach or ABME, absorption is uh, absorption metabolized something like that, and during the process the drug transporter is very important and the drug inside who is responsible for metabolize the drug is also very important so from the early stage the genetic information is just the focus of on the drug transporter or drug enzyme. These two kinds of things, yeah. Did I answer your question?

4. **Yuji:** Yes, thanks *<while nodding>*.

5. **Jiani:** Yes *<points to next person with a question>*.

6. **Tati:** Uh well is it, you're using genetic information, right?

7. **Jiani:** Yeah.

8. **Tati:** Doesn't it take a long time to analyze your genetic information?

9. **Jiani:** Do you mean how long does it take [**Tati:** Yeah] to do the genotyping?

10. **Tati:** Yeah.

11. **Jiani:** No, it's it's not that long, I think [**Yuji:** Um if I remember it correctly I think it just takes . . .] **Jiani:** Uh, I think less than one hour. Maybe we have another expert here, from biology. I think it's not too long.

12. **Tati:** Doesn't it depend on the method?

13. **Jiani:** Yeah.

14. **Tati:** So you're analyzing all the genetic information but you're taking some of the genetic information that you need . . . .

15. **Jiani:** Yeah especially for now especially for drug transporter and enzyme. *<pause>* Any more questions?

16. **Sojung:** Are there any *(unclear)* products?

17. **Jiani:** Any what?

18. **Sojung:** *(unclear)* products?

19. **Jiani:** Any products? Uh do you mean any drugs using this kind of technology right now?

20. **Sojung:** Yeah.

21. **Jiani:** Hmm, no, not now, not yet.

22. **Sojung:** I am just wondering because you said one problem in using the medications based on genotyping, is the side effects, I mean, what can you do about the problem of the side effects of the drugs . . . .

23. **Jiani:** Well I said there were four reasons for side effects *<gets overhead slide>* The last reason, the most important reason, is the population. So based on these reasons, somebody may not be a good fit for, for this drug since he or she was an infant. So based on the genetic information you can predict that this drug would help this person or harm this person. *<pause>* I think I didn't answer the question you asked . . . .

24. **Sojung:** Ahh . . . I guess I want to know if you can predict or avoid the side effects . . . .

25. **Jiani:** Okay, yeah I can give you example. Uh, for example for the, for the enzyme that's responsible for metabolizing the drug. Some people just uh don't have that kind of enzyme so he can not eliminate the drug, the drug just stays in the body it can not get out, he can't get rid of it, so this is the reason why he has the adverse drug reaction. And based on the genetic information we can tell in advance this person doesn't have that kind of enzyme so he can not take that particular drug. So, the person can avoid that drug and not have the adverse drug reaction. So he, this is just a very very simple example. Did that answer your question?

26. **Sojung:** Yeah.

27. **Jiani:** We can discuss this later if you want.

28. **Sojung:** Okay.

29. **Jiani:** Yeah. Okay. Time is up, uh thank you for your kind attention.

(Based on Academic Speaking. Student Presentation with Question/Answer session)

1. In your opinion, how successful was this Q&A session? Give an example of something that made it successful or not successful.

2. Find examples of the specific language the speaker uses in her Q&A and list them in the chart.

Q&A Strategies	Examples
Asks for questions from the audience	
Confirms whether the answer given was understood	
Asks for clarification	
Rephrases a question	
Indicates inability to answer	
Defers further discussion	
Indicates closing	

How do these examples compare to your examples from Task 21? Can you add any more examples in any category?

3. What can you do if an audience member starts to monopolize the Q&A, or asks an irrelevant question?

Guidelines for the Audience during Q & A Sessions

We often focus a great deal on how to answer questions, but what about your role in asking questions? Why is it important to ask questions? You may feel uncomfortable asking questions in a group situation, but just as with classroom participation, it is likely someone else in the group has the same question and will be glad you asked it. It is also awkward to have silence after the presenter initiates the Q&A. And, you may have observed how in some Q&A sessions, those asking the questions do so in order to show off a bit, and establish themselves as knowledgeable in the field. It could also be the case that in a classroom presentation, you are expected to ask questions (and maybe even graded on your participation). So, as a member of the audience at a panel or any presentation that has a question and answer session, there are a few things to remember when asking questions.

- Keep your question direct and to the point. Keep your questions relevant to the topic and content of the talk.
- If you intend to make a comment rather than ask a question, you can preface your statement by saying so. Comments can often encourage others to join a brief discussion.
- If the presenter is having a hard time catching your question because you are not loud enough, repeat the question in a stronger voice. Be sure you can be heard.
- If the presenter is having a hard time understanding your question and asks you to repeat, try to rephrase or use a different wording that might be clearer.
- Know when to give up. If your question just isn't being addressed, even after several attempts, suggest talking later, if the presenter doesn't suggest it first. Then, follow up with the presenter after the talk.

Using Visuals/Slides

Visual aids, such as overheads, PowerPoint, or other slides can greatly enhance a panel presentation if they are used appropriately. Visual outlines can provide organizational cues to both audience and speakers. Photos, charts, graphs, or maps can illustrate points quickly and concisely and can be very helpful if time is limited. Well-designed visuals, used effectively, can also engage the audience, keep its attention, and create a professional/polished image for the presenters. However, visuals that are overdone, for example, using "cute" graphics or excessive animation, can actually get in the way of the message. As a presenter you should ask yourself if you could get your message across without the visuals. Remember, they should supplement, not replace, your talk. Could the audience get your entire presentation just from reading your slides? If so, you need to rethink how you are using them.

Task 23

With your partner/group, evaluate the slides. Use the questions as a guide. If you feel the visuals could be improved, offer suggestions as to how they could be improved. Be ready to share your evaluation with the whole class.

- If there is an outline, is it clear? Is there too much or too little information?
- What kind of organizational pattern is being used?
- Are the font size and style of the text appropriate?
- Is there too much text on the slides?
- Are graphics used? If so, are they used appropriately? If not, what sort of graphics could be used to improve the visuals?
- Are charts, graphs, or tables used? Are they readable and clear?
- How could color be used to improve the visuals?

Example 1: Student slide presentation on *Alcohol Abuse on Campus*

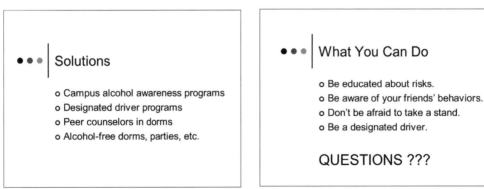

Example 2: First four slides from *Fostering Intercultural Communication* presentation

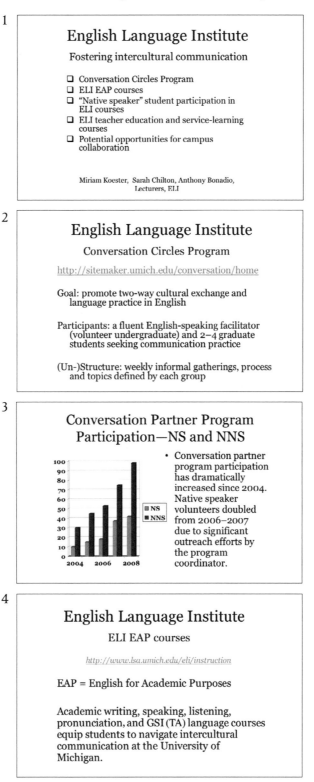

A common error presenters make is to not face the audience when using slides, over-heads, or a computer during their talk. The tendency is to look at and talk to the screen. It takes some practice to feel comfortable referring to slides, pointing by hand or using a laser pointer, while still addressing the audience. You also need to be sure you are not blocking the view of your slides.

How can you refer to the visuals you are using in your presentation? Let's look at some examples from MICASE where instructors are referring to slides, pictures, or maps.

Task 24

With your partner, underline any words in the examples that refer to visuals or refer to information on the visual. As a class, list phrases you can use in your presentations.

EXAMPLE 1: The anthropology professor is describing the locations on a map where the African language, Maa, is spoken.

> **Instructor:** So the Maa speakers *<pause>* as you can see uh this is a map of Kenya, and then down below is Tanzania, and the Maa speakers are the Ariaal you see them in the middle, the Ariaal, the Samburu, the Masai you see the Masai come all the way down into Tanzania. Um, and these are the communities that speak the Maa language. So it's spread over a wide area.
>
> (Based on MICASE. Intro Anthropology Lecture, File ID: LEL115JU090)

EXAMPLE 2: The physics professor is showing slides about the development of a particle accelerator.

> **Professor:** Now in this slide you see we started off as a little accelerator there in nineteen sixty-one, and gradually it became this one here . . . let's try to trace what happened going from there, to there. And the last thing I will say in this lecture will be about what happened using that machine. Okay? Now the next slide will show you what you see underground, . . .
>
> (Based on MICASE. Nobel Laureate Physics Lecture, File ID: COL485MX069)

EXAMPLE 3: The ecology professor, moving quickly through many slides, is describing a farm.

> **Professor:** . . . the next slide shows a slide from inside here. Uh and as you can see, there's a coconut tree here, there's uh, this is actually a a timber tree that was planted. Another timber tree that was planted there's fruit trees all over the place next slide shows a component of this system. This is the owner of the farm . . . next slide, shows a piece of the farm . . . .
>
> (Based on MICASE. Ecological Agriculture Colloquium, File ID: COL425MX075)

EXAMPLE 4: A natural sciences instructor is showing a picture of the area around the Huron River.

Instructor: Okay this shows a picture of the Huron watershed, and, all of these other, divisions are actually just sub-basins within this larger drainage basin, called the Huron watershed. And, I have another picture showing the particular outlet . . . so here we have every drop of water that falls within this area, gets drained out to this outlet right here.

(Based on MICASE. Spring Ecosystems Lecture, File ID: LES425SU093)

EXAMPLE 5: An art history instructor is describing historic photographs of a city.

Instructor: They were supposed to be tearing down unsanitary parts of the city. Um, and then instead putting in, wide new boulevards, like the one we see here lined with buildings in a uniform style, buildings that contain shops and apartment houses, um the streetscape was changing . . . .

(Based on MICASE. Renaissance to Modern Art History Lecture, File ID: LEL320JU143)

Add to this list of useful phrases for describing visuals.

As you can see	This is / This	The map shows
You see	That is / That	

DVD Task
Unit 6: Visuals
Scenes 1–2

In these scenes, two different instructors are describing a PowerPoint slide. The instructor in Scene 1 is not particularly prepared or skilled in presenting, while the instructor in Scene 2 has better presentation skills.

Watch both scenes without sound. Discuss the impact of the body language, gestures, movement, eye contact, and reference to the visual. List strengths and weaknesses of each presenter in these areas. Then, listen to the scenes with sound. List strengths and weaknesses in the presentation styles of the two instructors based on what they are saying.

Task 25

Practice presenting some visual information to the class or a small group of classmates. Talk for one to two minutes, then stop and ask your classmates/group to give you feedback on these points. If needed, repeat what you said, and talk for another minute or so, concentrating on making improvements based on the feedback.

Give feedback on:

- eye contact with audience
- voice projection/volume
- body position in relation to the visual
- pointing or indicating information on the visual
- language used to refer to the visual.

To practice, you can use an overhead, a slide printed out on paper, a poster, or map. Your instructor can provide examples or you can bring an example to class. You can talk about one of the visuals you evaluated in Task 23 or, if you are ready, use a visual that you will include in your final panel presentation.

Some Notes on Seating Arrangements and Equipment

Thinking about details like seating and equipment in advance will help your panel appear more prepared and professional. It is distracting for an audience to wait and watch while panel members try to figure out where to sit, in what order, where the equipment is, etc. It can also take up valuable time you should be spending presenting. Thus, when at all possible, spend some time before you are scheduled to present to check out the space and the equipment. This is illustrated in this MICASE example.

> **Instructor:** It's actually, really good practice when you're making an oral presentation before a group to do a dry run. [**Student**: Mhm] I mean it just really is. Th- there's so many, little picky things that can go wrong and after you've gotten everything put together it's such a shame to have those kinds of things mess you up. Um, but it happens, to everybody, at various times and uh unfortunately which is why I suggested that you bring a hard copy with you if, if it comes to that and we'll use the board and, you know go back to the old technology. Alright now what's the other group?
>
> (Based on MICASE. Politics of Higher Education Seminar, File ID SEM495SU111)

Typically panel members are seated in order of speaking, from the audience's left to right. Some presentations are given while seated; in others, each person will stand for his or her individual part. It may depend on where the computer is located if you are using one in your presentation.

Putting It All Together—Planning and Giving a Panel Presentation

Task 26

Prepare for panel presentations. Your instructor will provide details on your group assignment, the amount of time allowed for each presentation, and the schedule. Some of the steps in planning will take place in class, but you will need to meet outside of class as a group to prepare and practice. On the days that you will present your panel, other students and the instructor will be your audience, and they will provide written feedback to you.

Planning

Meet with your group. Your group may be assigned by the instructor or may be formed based on interest in a given topic.

Topics. Once you have decided on a topic, each person in the group should do some research. Bring one or two articles about your topic to class. As a group, share the information you have with each other. Your instructor will check to be sure each group has a different topic.

If you are not sure where to start, here are some possible topics to consider.

stress	alternative medicines
culture shock	English as a global language
prisoner rights	severe weather
instant messaging	wedding traditions
using laptops in college classrooms	information overload
cell phones	energy drinks
obesity	global warming
energy needs of countries	preserving historic buildings
computer games	protecting endangered species
medicine of the future	genetically modified foods
computer viruses	U.S. presidential election process

There are many ways to search online for information about the topics you are interested in. Your instructor can guide you to the appropriate libraries or resources on your campus. The reference librarians are excellent resources and can help with your research questions. You should find out about online databases and indexes as well as your school's online catalogue.

Content. Be sure you consider what your audience already knows when planning the content of your presentation. If you don't know, ask. If you spend too much time presenting basic information that everyone knows you risk boring your audience. Rather, you should quickly move to your new information so the audience will be interested and perhaps learn something from your presentation.

Organization. Decide how best to divide up the topic, and assign roles to each person. Decide who will be the facilitator and who will present the subtopics and in what order. You should carefully plan how you will start the presentation. It is helpful if the first speaker writes out the introduction to the panel. Write out the transitions between speakers. Each speaker should also write out the introduction to his or her own topic. Incorporate the organizational language and strategies you have learned in this unit.

Visuals. Decide what kinds of visuals you want and who will prepare them. With your instructor, discuss what equipment you will need (e.g., overhead projectors, computer projection, laptops, cables or adaptors, screens, etc.), and be sure your classroom is set up for your needs.

Practice and timing. It is very important to practice your parts individually and as a group, before the final presentation. It is important that you do not just read a prepared script. Try to work from note cards or an outline if you need something to refer to. Remember that visuals can serve as an outline for you. Do a final run-through, using the equipment and visuals and monitoring your time. Even if each of you have prepared well individually, the presentation might not be successful if, as a group, you are not prepared. Be ready to listen carefully to each other, and do not repeat information. Because there is usually a time limit for panels, make sure that everyone gets a chance to present. If one speaker takes too long, the others might not get a turn.

Preparing for questions. Anticipate the questions you might be asked individually or as a group.

Task 27

To prepare for your question and answer session, write three possible questions someone might ask you after hearing your presentation. In addition to simple clarification questions, think of questions that might challenge your point of view or question your data or research. You could do this task individually by focusing on your own part of the presentation, or work on it as a group to help each other come up with ideas.

Panel Presentation Feedback

After you finish your panel presentation, it is a good idea to reflect on how it went, what things went well, and what things could be improved. With the group, discuss the strengths and weaknesses of the presentation.

Pronunciation Focus: Difficult Consonant Sequences

Introduction

Consonant clusters consist of a series of two or three consonants in a row (e.g., the final three consonants in three-fourths and two-tenths). Consonant clusters can be difficult to pronounce—even for native speakers—if you try to say all of the consonant sounds. Therefore, typically not all the sounds are produced. Clusters can occur at word boundaries as well, which will affect pronunciation. For instance, in the fractions three-fourths and two-tenths, the *th* sound is typically dropped. In the *ststh* series in *I have three tests this week*, it is common to drop the final /t/ in *tests* and for some speakers the *th* sound as well. Here is another example:

    1. This month there are quizzes each week.

In the sequence *month there* the *th* in *month* and the *th* in *there* combine into one sound.

    However, in this next sentence the *th* sound is no longer pronounced as it is in isolation. Instead, the *th* sound may be dropped and only the final consonant of *is* (/z/) is pronounced.

    2. Is there any chance you could meet me today?

In this example, the /sks/ sequence is difficult to pronounce and so the /k/ may be dropped.

    3. Can we move the desks to form a circle?

In this last example, the /d/ may be dropped, possibly making it difficult to distinguish past tense from present tense without context.

    4. I rushed through the exam.

Data Collection and Analysis

Part 1: Transcription

With one or two partners, listen to Unit 6, Groups, Scene 1, 2, or 3 on the DVD, and then choose one to two minutes of speech to transcribe. Make sure that at least two turns contain some consonant clusters. Each of you should transcribe what you hear, listening to the DVD as many times as you need. You can listen together or individually. Once everyone is done transcribing, compare your transcriptions and try to create a complete transcript of the section you chose. Listen to the DVD again if necessary. Indicate any places in the recording where you cannot figure out what is being said and ask your instructor for some assistance.

Part 2: Analysis

With your partners, mark the difficult consonant sequences. Write your observations on these challenging sequences.

Part 3: Report to the class

Your report should provide the following information:

1. Remind your listeners of the focus of your investigation.
2. What, if anything, made it difficult to identify the consonant sequences. Was it the other words surrounding them? The recording? The speakers' rates of speaking? Characteristics of the speakers' pronunciations?
3. What are your group's observations on consonant sequences? What, if any, other interesting pronunciation observations did your group make?

Part 4: Production

With a partner, read aloud and/or role-play your transcript, paying special attention to consonant sequences.

References

Alfeld, Peter. "Do You Never Ask Questions in Class?" 1997. *http://www.math.utah.edu/~pa/math/a22.html* (accessed April 23, 2008).

Baron, M., ed. *Advising, Counseling and Helping the Foreign Student.* Washington, DC: National Association for Foreign Student Affairs, 1975.

Biesenbach-Lucas, S. "Communication Topics and Strategies in E-mail Consultation: Comparison between American and International University Students. *Language Learning and Technology* 9 (2005): 24–46.

Bippus, Amy M., Patricia Kearney, Timothy G. Plax, and Catherine F. Brooks. "Teacher Access and Mentoring Abilities: Predicting the Outcome Value of Extra Class Communication." *Journal of Applied Communication Research* 31 (2003): 260–75.

Bodine, Edward. "Getting the Most out of the U.S. Higher Education Experience: An Inside Perspective," 2005. *http://krakow.usconsulate.gov/krakow/inside2.html* (accessed April 15, 2008).

Bowal, Peter. "Speak Up in Class, Get a Better Education," 2000. *http://gauntlet.ucalgary.ca/story/7354* (accessed: April 16, 2008).

Boxer, Diana. *Complaining and Commiserating: A Speech Act View of Solidarity in Spoken American English.* New York: Peter Lang, 1993.

———. "Ethnographic Interviewing as a Research Tool in Speech Act Analysis: The Case of Complaints." In *Speech Acts across Cultures: Challenges to Communication in a Second Language,* edited by Susan M. Gass and Joyce Neu, 217–39. Berlin: Mouton, 1996.

Brown, P., and S. C. Levinson. *Politeness: Some Universals in Language Usage.* Cambridge, UK: Cambridge University Press, 1987.

Craig, B. L. "Variations and Themes in International Education." *Educational Record* 62 (1981): 41–46.

Crerar, Simon. "50 Craziest Celebrity Baby Names," 2007. *http://women.timesonline.co.uk/tol/life_and_style/women/families/article2130988.ece* (accessed April 25, 2008).

Crombie, Gail, Sandra W. Pike, Naida Silverthorn, Alison Jones, and Sergio Piccinin. "Students' Perception of Their Classroom Participation and Instructor as a Function of Gender and Context. *Journal of Higher Education* 74 (2003): 51–76.

Dyer, Judy, and Deborah Keller-Cohen. "The Discursive Construction of Professional Self through Narratives of Personal Experience." *Discourse Studies* 2 (2000): 283–304.

Edwards, Jane, and Humphrey R. Tonkin. "Internationalizing the Community College: Strategies for the Classroom." *New Directions for Community Colleges* 18 (1990): 17–26.

"Frequently Occurring First Names and Surnames from the 1990 Census." *www.census.gov/genealogy/www/freqnames.html* (accessed December 15, 2007).

"Frequently Occurring Surnames from Census 2000." *www.census.gov/genealogy/www/freqnames2k.html* (accessed June 23, 2008).

Fritschner, Linda Marie. "Inside the Undergraduate College Classroom: Faculty and Students Differ on the Meaning of Student Participation." *Journal of Higher Education* 71 (2000): 342–62.

Grice, H. P. "Logic and Conversation." In *Speech Acts,* edited by P. Cole and J. L. Morgan, 41–58. Vol. 3 of Syntax and Semantics. New York: Academic Press, 1975.

Lang, James M. "Office-Hour Habits of the North American Professor." *http://chronicle.com/jobs/2003/05/2003051301c.htm* (accessed April 16, 2008).

Leech, Geoffrey N. *Principles of Pragmatics.* London: Longman, 1983.

Levin, Peter. "Team Virgins Fear an Orgy of Togetherness." *The Times Higher Education* (Aug. 15, 2003): 22.

Limberg, H. "Discourse Structure of Academic Talk in University Office Hour Interactions." *Discourse Studies* 9 (2007): 176–93.

Nicol, David J., and James T. Boyle. "Peer Instruction versus Class-wide Discussion in Large Classes: A Comparison of Two Interaction Methods in the Wired Classroom." *Studies in Higher Education* 28 (October 2003): 457–73.

"Popular Baby Names." *www.ssa.gov/OACT/babynames* (accessed February 1, 2008).

Sahay, Apratim. "University of Chicago Prospective Students Advisory Committee (PSAC)'s International Student Profiles," 2006. *http://psac.uchicago.edu/profiles/tim.html* (accessed April 16, 2008).

Sanders, Martin. "A Failure to Collaborate." *Chronicle of Higher Education* (Feb. 22, 2008): 54.

Tracy, Ben. "Good Question: Why Do We Have Middle Names?" *http://wcco.com/goodqueslocaltion/_story_180084214.html* (accessed May 15, 2007).

Weaver, Robert R., and Jiang Qi. "Classroom Organization and Participation: College Students' Perceptions." *Journal of Higher Education* 76 (2005): 570–601.

Academic Interactions DVD Contents and Track Times